What people are saying about Pursuing the Mystery of Christ

In *Pursuing the Mystery of Christ*, Steve Stewart models the rare wisdom of recognizing and bowing to Mystery when he sees it. With humility, curiosity, and persistent hunger, this seasoned practitioner of kingdom ministry turns his heart and mind to wonder about the nature of the same Christ he has served and worshiped and witnessed for many decades. For Steve, the Incarnation is not a theological theory to be dissected or abstracted... and certainly not mastered. Rather, the Incarnation is a Person he knows intimately and loves with his whole life. Now, through Steve's eyes and pen, and the help of his Patristic mentors, we glimpse the meaty Reality of the Word who became flesh, even if as in a mirror dimly.

Bradley Jersak (PhD Theology)
President, St. Stephen's University, NB Canada
Author of A More Christlike Trilogy

The first time I met Steve the heart of the Father and the legacy for impacting nations was totally evident. *Pursuing the Mystery of Christ* invites us to lift the lid off the boxes that our limited experience can sometimes contain Him in. It reveals the hope that we carry on the inside of us to experience the unlimited power of our limitless God, increasing our hunger to know the wonders of His person.

Kim Jones
Senior Leader, Liberty Family Church,
Australia

Papa Steve has spent decades truly knowing Christ... deeply. Then more deeply. Then more deeply still. This book, decades in the making, is a game changer. It introduces us to the eternal, cosmic and complete representation of God, the final Word about what God has to say about Himself, the Word of God, Jesus of Nazareth. It will leave you in hot pursuit of the eternal mystery revealed in Jesus Christ. The One who was from the beginning, who was from before the foundations of the world, and who is from everlasting to everlasting.

Craig Stephens
New Expressions Coordinator, The Salvation Army,
Australia

Steve Stewart is a man who refuses to rest on the past laurels of his personal encounters with Christ. In *Pursuing the Mystery of Christ,* Steve will inspire you to explore the wonder of the ever-unfolding mystery of Christ. Embracing the mystery of the Gospel will open your imagination to see just how vast and inclusive God's Kingdom really is.

Steve Smothers
Author, Lead Equipping Pastor, Sozo Church,
United States

In *Pursuing the Mystery of Christ* the writer takes us both deep and wide in this lifelong pursuit. We will never fully know or understand. It's big. He's big. Steve has a deep desire to know Christ beyond mere information, leading to a profound experience of his transcendent and immanent nature. You will be both encouraged and challenged, and through the Holy Spirit discover more of the mystery of Christ.

Miriam Gluyas
Territorial Commander, Chair of the Board
The Salvation Army Australia Territory

For me, a good book must leave me in awe of God – and this book hits that target right in the heart. *Pursuing the Mystery of Christ* draws from the history of the church making the ancient come to life, its heart felt connecting to the present now – and brings the reader along on a journey into deeper fullness as to the nature of Jesus. All in all leaving the reader in awe of the God-Man Jesus Christ.

Murray Dueck
President of Samuel's Mantle Training Society, Canada

I've had the joy and delight of sitting under Steve's ministry in the dusty villages of India and in the carpeted cathedral of our church in Sydney. And each time what pours out of him is Jesus. Jesus the Man, the Mystery, the Manifestation of hope and salvation. Delve into these pages, linger a bit, let Christ fill you even deeper than you dreamt possible. What you've longed for is not far off, He's closer than you think.

Fini de Gersigny
Senior Pastor & Co-founder, Jubilee Church Sydney,
Songwriter
Australia

Pursuing the Mystery of Christ is a most wonderful book! It treats the subject of its title in a kaleidoscopic manner, with a clearly-written and beautiful flow. Everything is thoroughly referenced – spanning from the Old Testament, on through the New Testament, and extending to the Church Fathers and Mothers. As one reads *Pursuing the Mystery of Christ*, a vector of increasing length forms in the reader's mind and spirit that point directly to the Cross, which is the topic of Steve's next book, *Pursuing the Mystery of the Cross*. After that Steve intends to write a third book, *Pursuing the Mystery of the Trinity*. It is my opinion that this trilogy is destined to become a classic of Christian literature.

Charles M. Beck II
BS Chemistry, Worcester Polytechnic Institute,
MDiv Theology, Princeton Theological Seminary

PURSUING
the MYSTERY *of*
CHRIST

STEVE STEWART

USA/Canada ISBN: 9798884037922
Australia ISBN: 979-8-8692-9898-0
© 2024 by Steve Stewart

Impact Nations Publishing
PO Box 45596
Rio Rancho, NM 87124

Unless otherwise noted, Scripture quotations are taken from the New Revised Standard Version (NRSV)

New Kings James Version	NKJV
King James Version	KJV
Septuagint (OSB)	LXX
New International Version	NIV
New Century Version	NCV
Christian Standard Bible	CSV
New Living Translation	NLT
English Standard Version	ESV
New American Standard Bible	NASB

To contact the author or order copies, visit
www.impactnations.com

DEDICATION

When Christ first planted in my heart the nucleus of what would become Impact Nations, I never imagined that it would lead to an ever-growing, wonderful, and multi-national family. I dedicate this book to the sons and daughters around the world whose vision, courage, and remarkable dedication to the Lord are continually advancing the Kingdom of Heaven. You have taken the bits of bread and fish that I placed in your hands and watched them multiply in powerful and creative ways as you have given them away. I am so thankful and proud of each one of you.

Mark 1:11

Table of Contents

Foreword 1

Introduction: Unsearchable Riches 7

1. Christ Beyond Time, Space and Matter 25

2. Christ in Creation 47

3. Christ in the Old Testament 71

4. Into The Heart of the Mystery 93

5. The Incarnation, Part Two 115

6. Established in His Humanity 135

7. Mystery in Ministry 157

8. The Glory of Christ 181

9. The Final Mountain 207

Epilogue 235

Acknowledgements 239

Foreword

The Enlightenment of the seventeenth century ushered in the epoch of empiricism—or what Thomas Paine called the "Age of Reason." On the first page of his influential book, *The Age of Reason: Being an Investigation of True and Fabulous Theology*, first published in 1794, Thomas Paine confidently asserted, "My own mind is my own church." We almost have to admire Paine's supreme self-assuredness, but we also need to admit that one's own mind makes for an uncomfortably small church. Rather than the brash attempt to confine God to the intellect, we are better served by the wisdom of Solomon when he humbly prayed, "the heaven of heavens cannot contain Thee." But such was the hubris of the time. There is a direct line from René Descartes as a devout Catholic positing, "I think, therefore I am," to Thomas Paine as an irreligious Deist boasting, "My own mind is my own church."

It is probably worth noting that what would become evangelicalism was born in the Age of Reason and rocked in the cradle of empiricism. Obviously, the evangelical theology that eventually emerged in the nineteenth and twentieth centuries did not reject Christianity as

Thomas Paine did, but it did capitulate to the terms set by the Cartesian and empiricist projects of modernity. Evangelical thought more or less assumed that all that can be known about God and the phenomenon of being could be ascertained though something resembling scientific method. There was to be no room for mystery. Mystery was to be recast as mere ignorance and discarded with medieval superstition. As in the Sherlock Holmes mystery novels of the time—in which there was actually no mystery, only riddles—it was now all "elementary, my dear Watson."

At the beginning of the twentieth century, evangelical theology, in reaction to what it perceived as a mortal threat in Darwinism, moved steadily toward fundamentalism. It unwittingly accepted the terms of empiricism and began to treat Scripture as a scientific text whose mysteries could be unraveled by pseudo-scientific methods. Thus was born the wrongheaded project of "proving" the Bible. Fundamentalist apologetics inspired expeditions to Mount Ararat in search of Noah's ark, while others scuba-dived in the Red Sea in search of Pharaoh's chariots. The Bible had become an infallible but imperiled text that had to be defended by empirical proof. This is the folly that would eventually help launch a million "deconstructions." Fundamentalism is filled with trap doors tumbling down into atheism.

Meanwhile, the more liberal-minded Protestants who, unlike their fundamentalist cousins, were not in reaction to the scientism of modernity, began to actively court it. And thus was born the many quests for the historical Jesus. Instead of climbing Mount Ararat or diving in the

Red Sea, their expedition would be into Scripture itself via historical-critical textual analysis. And here it must be admitted that this was by far the more fruitful of the two endeavors. There is real benefit in exploring the biblical text as a literary document that has a definite and somewhat identifiable origin story. There is tremendous value in attempting to understand Jesus of Nazareth in the context of his time—a Second Temple period Galilean Jew living under the hegemony of the Roman Empire. But this also has its absurd side. One thinks of the antics of the "Jesus Seminar" with their self-important press conferences smugly announcing to reporters that the historical Jesus certainly didn't do this or say that. They should have concluded each press conference by saying, "Our own mind is our own church." At the end of the day, modern theological fundamentalism and theological liberalism are two sides of the same empiricist coin.

But the biggest problem with these modern approaches, be they the pop apologetics of fundamentalism or the scholarly endeavors of the historical-critical method, is that one will never actually encounter the sacred mystery that is responsible for the religious interest in the first place. Even if an adventurer does dig up gopherwood on Mount Ararat or an archeologist unearths an actual "Q source" parchment, so what? All you really have is a bit of wood or piece of paper. Ultimately, the only reason for going to the effort of trekking up a Turkish mountain or excavating ancient archives is because Scripture itself points to a sacred mystery beyond itself—a sacred mystery that Christianity confesses we are invited to participate in. This is the mystery of Christ we are to pursue.

Steve Stewart is a veteran Christian leader who thankfully did not get stuck in the blind alley of fundamentalism or wander off into the cul-de-sac of liberalism but found the way forward by pursuing the mystery of Christ. Steve Stewart's story resonates with me. In midlife, after two decades of pastoral ministry, I had a mystical experience in the Rocky Mountains that alerted me to the truth that the greatest wonder of all is this: the Word became flesh and dwelt among us. This is the mystery of Christ. And pursuing this mystery saved me from the soul-crushing disenchantment that stalks our secular age. Of course to part with the enforced certitude that is but a crude caricature of authentic faith is to invite criticism. I'm sure Steve has been charged with "going liberal" by some who fancy themselves as theological police. But an honest reading of *Pursuing The Mystery of Christ* would disabuse anyone of this silly notion. Throughout the book, Steve engages with a host of church fathers—Christianity's first theologians who represent the true nature of what actually constitutes a conservative approach to theology. At the heart of a true conservative theology is a high Christology; and the higher our Christology, the greater the mystery of Christ. The point of knowing Christ through revelation and sacrament is not to "solve" Christ in rationalism, but to encounter Christ in mystery.

For Steve Stewart, the church is not his own mind but the Church—the whole church with its long historical depth and broad ecumenical width. In *Pursuing The Mystery of Christ* you will hear theological voices from the entire spectrum of Christian tradition—Orthodox, Catholic, Anglican, Protestant, and Pentecostal voices are all present. Ancient and contemporary Christian thinkers are all equally engaged. In this book academic theology comfortably mixes with modern mystical experiences. On one page Scottish Presbyterian theologian T.F. Torrance is cited and on another page you will find personal accounts of the miraculous. This represents the kind of Christianity that has a future. This is the re-enchantment the disenchanted Christian soul longs for. Instead of settling for paper-thin modern evangelicalism or engaging in endless postmodern deconstruction, Steve Stewart wisely invites us to pursue the mystery of Christ.

Brian Zahnd
Author of *When Everything's on Fire* and *The Wood Between the Worlds*

Unsearchable Riches

"To me, who am less than the least of all the saints, this grace was given, that I should preach among the Gentiles the unsearchable riches of Christ, and to make all see what is the fellowship of the mystery, which from the beginning of the ages has been hidden in God who created all things through Jesus Christ." (Eph 3:8-9 NKJV)

From his first encounter with Christ on the Damascus Road, Paul's life, vision and focus was centered upon the mystery of Christ. The longer Paul gazed upon Christ, the more magnificent and all-encompassing he became. It was the same for the twelve disciples. As their experience of Jesus grew from anointed teacher to healer, deliverer and miracle worker who even commanded the elements, they asked one another in wonder (and I suspect some fear), "What manner of man *is* this?"

Pursuing Christ and experiencing mysteries beyond our understanding are inseparable. The mystery of Christ is like nothing else in the cosmos; its pursuit directs our lives toward a limitless, ever-changing, ever-deepening treasure, beyond all measures of value. For this treasure, this Christ-mystery, leads us to the Eternally Beautiful One.

"Faith in Christ, and in the mysteries of His life and death, is the foundation of the Christian life and the source of all contemplation: and about this there can be no doubt."[1]

Often, we find these mysteries too uncomfortable, causing us to retreat to what feels like a safer and surer place. Yet, when we allow ourselves to face existential uncertainty with all its questions and dissembling of what we thought we knew about God, we embark on the greatest journey of discovery offered to humankind: the limitless riches of Christ.

"Art is so often better at theology than theology is, because it is more willing to face the silence and the 'unmeaning'—those aspects of God and our own existence that simply lie beyond our reach, ungraspable and unmasterable."[2]

The Enlightenment's Hold

Much of the western church long ago pulled back from embracing mystery, or even from the awareness of it. Paul spoke of mystery twenty-one times—the New Testament twenty-eight times—yet how often have we heard sermons about the mystery of Christ? Instead of mystery, we present principles and propositional truth, as though the Bible is something that with enough study, we can

---

1   Thomas Merton, *New Seeds of Contemplation*, (New Directions Publishing Co., 2007) p.152

2   Chris E.W. Green, *All Things Beautiful*, (Baker University Press, 2021) p.26

figure out, molding it to fit our purposes. Sometimes, the Triune God himself is presented in the same rationalistic way. Perhaps even more than *ignoring* the mystery of the Gospel, we have come to the place where we *avoid* it.

I remember a number of years ago being in a coffee shop with a fellow pastor. As we chatted, he looked over at another table and saw a young man reading a book by a well known contemplative author. My friend's response was immediate, almost visceral, as he warned me that the book was heresy and should be avoided. In fact, this Christian author's books have encouraged and deepened my own walk with Jesus for a long time. I bring this up to illustrate the almost instinctive fear that many Christians have for anything that is beyond their familiar, defined boundaries of who Jesus is and what it means to be a believer. Anthony Ugolnik addresses the Western church's tendency to avoid the essential mysterious nature of Christianity: "We Christians in the West confess we have not shared what we possess. We have mystery in plenty yet our discourse avoids it as if in embarrassment."[3]

It would be impossible to overstate the impact of the Enlightenment of the 17th and 18th centuries upon every part of our lives. While its gift was to free the western culture from previous centuries of being controlled by superstition, the Enlightenment limited our spiritual worldview by validating only what could be perceived through the five senses. Rationalism continues today to be the core value and belief system that dominates and conditions all

---

3   Cited by Christopher A. Hall, *Learning Theology With the Church Fathers*, InterVarsity Press, 2002) p.10

of our institutions and the media to which we are exposed almost every waking moment. We seek knowledge as our greatest value, never more so than in the rapidly accelerating information age in which we all live; but it must be empirical and observable. This has dominated our approach to theology. For over 150 years the historical-critical method of reading Scripture has reigned supreme in evangelical circles. It assumes that with enough research we can know the historical intent of the original author (if we can agree on who that actually is!) and on how their words were understood by their audience. The scriptural passage can mean no more and no less. This has led to a very "two dimensional" reading of Scripture, precluding the possibility that the Holy Spirit continues to speak new truths through ancient verses. The historical-critical method denies the nuances, the multi-layered meanings of Scripture that have been at the heart of its theological study for nearly two thousand years.

A Safe Gospel is a Small Gospel

The result of approaching the Bible in this way has led to a Gospel that has gradually become safer and more predictable. A Gospel largely without wonder is tame and understandable, something that we can get our minds around. Perhaps the greatest loss is to be left with a small Gospel that does not stir heart-wonder, or even capture the interest of the world around us. A Gospel that isn't big enough to illuminate, to bring meaningful here-and-now hope to people. A Gospel that does not reach beyond time and space, to a universe that pulses with the infinite life of Christ.

Will we embrace, and allow ourselves to be embraced by, a limitless, never-to-be-fully-understood Gospel that is full of both wonder and risk? Will we turn our attention and affections to pursue that which is, paradoxically, boundless beyond our boundaries, unknowable beyond what we will ever know. "This mystery is not a puzzle that baffles; it is an infinity to explore."[4]

A Gospel without mystery and wonder inevitably points to a Jesus who came to earth so that I could go to heaven, instead of the One who holds the entire cosmos together, who is in all things and has created all things. The small gospel that is so often preached today can be reduced to the invitation to "Come to Jesus. Come to church. Be good. Go to heaven." I expect the early church would not have even recognized this gospel, for the gospel that they both received and proclaimed rocked the Roman world: Christ's death and resurrection has made everything new. The old has passed away; we have entered the beginning of eternal life *right now* (2 Cor 5:17; Rev 21;1-50).

As the church father Gregory of Nyssa wrote long ago, "God's name is not known; it is to be wondered at." Without mystery, there is no awe, no astonishment. Without these we are left with a series of principles to learn. Without mystery there is no true movement toward the Triune God.

---

4   Eugene Peterson, *Reversed Thunder*, (Harper San Francisco 1988) p.40

God, the Gospel, and Imagination

But is the Gospel truly beautiful, able to capture our hearts and minds, with power to transport our imaginations? Even asking this question pushes some of us beyond our safe comfort zones, causing us to ask, "What has imagination got to do with the truth of the Gospel? Doesn't such thinking open us up to error?" Einstein said, "The imagination is more important than intelligence, meaning there can be no meaningful use of intelligence unless there is imaginative perception."

Imagination and creation seem to be two sides of the same coin. Surely God imagined before he spoke the cosmos into being. Any pursuit of Christ's unsearchable riches must take us on a journey of imagination, rooted in the scriptures and in the tradition of those who have gone before, but one of *experiencing* beyond what we have known heretofore. Eugene Peterson, describing the adventure of reading Revelation, wrote: "Our imaginations are kindled with a vision—of Christ. We are roused, attentive, alert. Everything is suddenly in proportion."[5]

Jesus Christ is fully God. Not one who points to God. Not one like God. He is God. And as we shall see, God is love. Full stop. Everything about Christ, everything that he has done, is doing, and will do is an expression of his love. From the beginning of the universe, all that he has created declares the infinite, boundless and mysterious love of Christ. And in the eternal "now," he constantly and continually loves all that he has created. As King David wrote, "Such knowledge is too wonderful for me." (Ps 139:6)

---

5   Peterson, *Reversed Thunder*, p.28

There is a tendency to think that the mystery of Christ began with the Incarnation, but no, it does not begin with an angelic visitation to a young peasant girl named Mary. From its earliest days, the church understood that Christ is in *all* of scripture—that Adam and Eve, Abraham, Jacob, Moses, Joshua, Gideon and beyond had personal encounters with Christ. Not only do we see him in the Biblical past; the Old Testament points forward to, and contains, the revelation of Christ. As Ignatius, an early church father who sat at the feet of the Apostle John, wrote:

> "But for me the archives [Old Testament] are Jesus Christ, the inviolable archives are His cross and death and His resurrection and the faith which is through Him … He is the door of the Father through which enter Abraham and Isaac and Jacob and the prophets and the apostles and the church."[6]

While it is of great value to consistently read the four Gospels, since they reveal the One who we are invited to follow, there is a danger of overlooking who the second Person of the Trinity really is, limiting him to his words and actions in the four Gospel accounts. As we begin to recognize Jesus Christ throughout the entire Bible, our eyes are open to see him everywhere—even *beyond* space and time.

Paul declared his calling to proclaim the mystery of the unsearchable riches of Christ (Eph 3:8-9). What does

---

6   St. Irenaeus, *On the Apostolic Preaching*, translated by John Behr, (St. Vladimir's Seminary Press, 1997) p.10

scripture mean by "mystery"? It is a divine secret that is revealed by God in his perfect time for our understanding; although we can never fully understand this mystery, it leads us onward into greater depths of God. This is not something that we can deduce through our own efforts; it is a grace gift. Mystery is filled with the paradox of seemingly contrary truths held in tension; it carries us beyond the safe bounds of what we are sure we know.

Transcendence and Immanence

Two great truths about God revolve around the paradox of his otherness (transcendence) and his nearness (immanence). Eight hundred years ago the Irish mystic and theologian John Scotus Eriugena wrote,

> "Mystery, while remaining unknown, makes the unknown known. By mystery, the transcendent is introduced into our world and becomes immanent while remaining ever transcendent."[7]

The Triune God is beyond us in every way; he is transcendent. He is both the creator of everything and distinct from all he has created, beyond the cosmos of matter, space and time. He is not confined by the universe. The Nicene Creed declares that he is the creator of all that is seen and unseen. God is transcendent in his holiness, sinlessness and power. To claim to understand the One who is infinitely and eternally beyond us will inevitably

---

7   John Scotus Eriugena, *The Voice of the Eagle, translated by Christopher Bamford* (Lindisfame Books, 2000) p.174

lead to fashioning an idol made in our own image—the antithesis of transcendent.

> "Any god who is mine but not yours, a god
> concerned with me but not with you, is an idol."[8]

Secondly, God is immanent. The transcendent God of mystery is always filling all things (Eph 1:23). Christ is present everywhere around us and within us. There is no place without Christ. The God who is infinitely beyond our understanding reveals himself as Person. As St. Augustine famously said, "He is closer to me than I am to myself." He calls us by name, inviting us into an eternal relationship. At the heart of this invitation is his constant, unwavering love. Pursuing the mystery of Christ will always carry us along on both an outward and inward journey.

> "There exists with Him a single love and compassion
> which is spread out over all creation, a love which is
> without alteration, timeless, and everlasting."[9]

Everywhere is his love—both the foundation and the movement of the cosmos. When I move in love, I discover that I am moving in the true rhythm of life, because it is *his* rhythm.

> *In Him we live and move and have our being.*
> *(Acts 17:28)*

---

8   Abraham Heschel, *Religion and Race,* (https://www.blackpast.org/african-american-history/1963-rabbi-abraham-joshua-heschel-religion-and-race)

9   Alvin Kimel, *Destined for Joy,* (self published 2022 ISBN 9798841664772) p.3

Because Christ is in me, in pursuing his riches I discover and learn to recognize my truest self. And because of his otherness, I am caught up in the truth of how wide, how long, how high, and how deep is the love of Christ that creates and sustains all things for all time.

How can it be that the God who is bigger and beyond all of creation is the One who knows, loves, and woos me to himself? Isaiah presents us with a picture of the transcendence and immanence of God:

> *For thus says the High and Lofty One*
> *Who inhabits eternity, whose name is Holy:*
> *"I dwell in the high and holy place,*
> *With him who has a contrite and humble spirit,*
> *To revive the spirit of the humble,*
> *And to revive the heart of the contrite ones."*
> *(Is 57:15, NKJV)*

God is both further away and nearer than anything or anyone else. Surely, this is a mystery that we will never fully comprehend.

The creation of the universe reveals the infinite love of the Triune God; as a musical piece expresses the heart of the composer, so creation is the song, the symphony, that endlessly declares the nature of its Creator. That which he has called into being and formed is the object of his heart's desire. It is not a distant love, but a very personal, even passionate love for all he has made, and that, of course, includes you and me. God's love was never more personally and powerfully expressed than through the Incarnation, when the Creator became part of his creation.

Embracing Mystery's Darkness

"We see through a glass, darkly" (1 Cor 13:12, KJV)

While we may imagine that pursuing the mystery of Christ will lead to greater clarity and light, instead we encounter the paradox of the journey. As Christ grows before the eyes of our heart, we are faced with more mysteries, not less. He dwells in unapproachable light (1 Ti 6:16), yet at times seems to hide himself in darkness (Ps 97:2).

This has always been so. Abraham first heard God speak to him, calling him out from the known of Ur, where he has lived his whole life, to the unknown of "a land that I will show you." This is the pattern experienced in the pursuit of deep relationship with Christ. Abraham moved from the known environment of Ur, one of the great cities of ancient times where he and his ancestors had lived for generations, to Haran, a city that was merely a transitory place, and then on to the distant and unknown land of Canaan. In spite of his faith, in many ways, Abraham's obedience led to more seasons of perplexity than clarity. In Genesis 15 God calls Abraham out into the darkness to show him a vision of the future. Genesis recounts that "Abram believed God, and He counted it to him for righteousness." This was so important that it was recorded throughout the New Testament. With Abraham's faith and obedience established, now his life and relationship with God would surely become clearer. Not so much. Within hours, again with darkness as the backdrop, "a trance fell upon Abram; and behold, horror and great darkness fell upon him." As God consecrates his covenant, it is in the midst of a flame, a smoking oven, and lamps of fire.

The darkness and smoke speak of Abraham's ongoing journey with this God of mystery. (There isn't anything much more mysterious than being told to kill his son Isaac, the child of promise!)

And yet, with all of the uncertainties, the times of both confusion and despair, something kept pulling Abraham forward. Christ had hooked his heart. This friend of God had grown to trust the grace-voice of the One who continued to speak in the depths of his heart: "I am always with you; I am always for you." Centuries later, Jesus would ask his disciples if they, like so many others, were going to leave him too. Peter answered, "Where else could we go? You've shown us eternal life. We're hooked. We've seen and lived too much to ever turn back." Abraham's experience was the same.

> *By faith Abraham obeyed when he was called to set out for a place that he was to receive as an inheritance; and he set out, not knowing where he was going. By faith he stayed for a time in the land he had been promised, as in a foreign land, living in tents, as did Isaac and Jacob, who were heirs with him of the same promise. For he looked forward to the city that has foundations, whose architect and builder is God. (Heb 11:8-10)*

From light to darkness; from certainty to mystery. This is the nature of the journey of pursuing the unsearchable riches of Christ. If we look closely we see the pattern emerge again with Moses.

"He caused [Moses] to hear His voice,
Then led him into the darkness."
(Wisdom of Sirach 45:5 LXX)

He first encountered Christ, the second Person of the Trinity, as a burning bush, its strange light drawing Moses closer. Soon, Moses and the Israelites will encounter Christ as both a pillar of light and of cloud; this is a picture of the Lord drawing us from what we think we know to the unknowable. On Mount Sinai the Lord gives Moses the foundational laws for relationship with Him and with one another—the Ten Commandments. The setting is vitally important. When God came down upon Mount Sinai, it was with supernatural "thunderings, the lightning flashes, the sound of the trumpet, and the mountain smoking." No wonder the people stood back in terror. As the Lord calls Moses to come up, it is a call into darkness: "Moses drew near the thick darkness where *God was.*" (Ex 20:21)

Pilgrimages are both exciting and unsettling, exposing us to new experiences, new realities. Around every bend there is the potential for things we have never encountered before. They increase our horizons and can change the way we see the world. Spiritual pilgrimages are no different. But they are not just about the excitement of experiencing what is new. Along the way we are confronted with our idols. Perhaps the most unsettling idol of all is the God we have created in our own preferred and predictable image. As George Bernard Shaw once wrote, "God created mankind in His own image, and ever since, man has been returning the favor."

Mystery and Faith

Pursuing the mystery of Christ, if we allow it, will lead us again and again into repentance. This is not necessarily about weeping at the altar, but more about changing the assumptions we carry with us about ourselves, others and Christ. This is the true meaning of repentance—*metanoia*: to turn around or to change our way of thinking. At a deep level, we are afraid to abandon our certainties about God in order to follow him in his true and mysterious self. If we allow questions to creep in, will they somehow lead to the destruction of our entire faith? If we are honest, we much prefer to hold onto what we think we know about who Christ is. This is why, in our churches, we hear so little about the mystery of Christ. Mystery confronts the boundaries of our doctrine.

We live in a time when there are two great forces at work among followers of Jesus. There is a growing movement of men and women who are asking questions about how their faith has been formed. These are significant questions with huge implications. For some, these have ultimately led to walking away from Christianity, as they have experienced it, or even from relationship with Christ. For others, questions have led to a re-forming of how they live out their faith. The other current force in the church is to double down on doctrine, to insist on the traditions of one's denomination. In this environment, where proclamation of certainties abound, there is very little room for pursuing the unsearchable riches of Christ.

Faith is central to our relationship with the Lord; it has been called the currency of the Kingdom. True faith is *not* shutting ourselves from the unknown or unfamiliar. Faith is about having more confidence in the Holy Spirit's ability to lead us into truth, than in Satan's capacity to deceive us. True and authentic faith, like Abraham's, propels me forward to meet the unfamiliar. It is built upon a deep confidence that it is Jesus himself who is inviting and drawing me on this sojourn into the unknown. It is this gift of faith that stirs an unquenchable thirst and, as the Apostle John wrote, "We love because he first loved us." (1 Jn 4:19) This spiritual journey is all about Jesus; our entry is through personal love. This is the motivation, the means and the movement of the pilgrimage. It is not about esoteric experiences, like modern day Gnostics. The journey is about the infinite love of Christ. This divine love is:

> "an endless revelation of the Divinity in his creative
> act. Divine love lies at the foundation of the universe,
> it governs the world, and it will lead the world
> to that glorious outcome when it will be entirely
> 'consumed' by the Godhead."[10]

Pursuing the Secret Call

Pursuing Christ, and in him, the Triune God, is my response to the secret call within me. It is a marker, telling me that my longing for something more, for something eternal, something that touches the infinite, is an assurance that it is Christ who is calling me into

---

10   Hiiarion Alfeyev, *The Spiritual World of Isaac the Syrian*, (Cisterian Publications, 2000) p.37

uncharted territory with him. The secret call is a precious gift, one deserving of much prayer and contemplation. It is never to be shrugged off as wishful thinking or unrealistic. The secret call is an invitation into our truest self, which we can only discover in Christ.

> "The human being is nothing less than insatiable thirst for the divine, an inspirited ever-seeking for the One who is our completion and fulfillment."[11]

As much as we hunger for Christ, his longing for us is greater. And so, he encourages us to keep on asking, seeking, knocking. Along the way, when we become tired, discouraged, or simply distracted, his unwavering love continues to draw us. Among the many sustaining promises for this journey are the words of Isaiah:

> *Your eyes will see the king in his beauty and view a land that stretches afar. (Is 33:17 NIV)*

When we encounter the beauty of Christ, touching our center, we begin to see the world around us in new ways, awakened to its beauty, a reflection and expression of the One who made everything. The love and beauty of Christ are not only the foundation, they are the nexus of time and space, of the cosmos from which all things find their meaning. As the medieval theologian, John Scotus Eriugena wrote: "Every visible or invisible creature is a theophany or appearance of God." Pursuing the mystery of Christ opens our eyes to recognize his nearness and loveliness in those around us. We are surprised to

---

11 Kimel, *Destined for Joy*, p.310

discover that we are experiencing Christ through others. Another paradox: this very personal interior journey brings us into a much greater interconnection with the world around us, something we never anticipated.

Christ *Is* the Mystery

As we have seen, mystery is foundational to much of the New Testament. The Apostle Paul was very much a mystic. While many of us have thought that mysticism is something ethereal or unattainable, a Christian mystic is anyone who places experiencing God personally as their number one priority, as opposed to simply knowing about God in Scripture, church doctrine and theology.[12] Paul interpreted life from an eternal, heavenly perspective.

> *He has made known to us the mystery of his will,*
> *according to his good pleasure that he set forth in Christ,*
> *as a plan for the fullness of time, to gather up all things in*
> *him, things in heaven and things on earth. (Eph 1:9-10)*

Mystery is a divine secret that is revealed by God in his perfect time. Although we can never fully understand this mystery, it leads us onward into greater depths of God. It is not something that we can deduce through our own efforts; it is a grace gift. Paul understood that God's plan and purpose for the fullness of time was the revelation of Christ coming to us.

Christ is not only the One who reveals the Triune mystery; he is himself that mystery.

---

12   Richard Rohr, *What the Mystics Know*, (Crossroad Pub, 2019)

I want them to be strengthened and joined together with love so that they may be rich in their understanding. This leads to their knowing fully God's secret, that is, Christ himself. (Col 2:2 NCV)

In Eph 1:10 Paul tells us that the mystery of Christ is of such inconceivable magnitude that it is at the center of the "summing up of all things" both on earth and in heaven. The final destiny of the cosmos is perfect unity, the ultimate fulfillment of God's great plan.

Christ is the truth at the core of all creation. The mystery of Christ is what gives meaning to all of life: meaning to your life and mine, meaning to every life on this planet, and meaning to the universe itself. Because of this great mystery, all of the ages and beings of time and space—all of the ever-expanding universe—receive their beginning and end in Christ. He has brought together the infinite and the finite; the visible and the invisible; the Creator and creation—unsearchable, unfathomable riches.

Our revelation of the Gospel can only be as big as our revelation of Christ. It is my hope that as we behold the beauty of the King, as we pursue the unfathomable, we will discover that he has given us a Gospel that is bigger and more multi-dimensional than we ever imagined. It is the Gospel for which all of creation was made.

CHAPTER ONE

Christ Beyond Time, Space and Matter

He is the image of the invisible God, the firstborn over all creation. For everything was created by Him, in heaven and on earth, the visible and the invisible, whether thrones or dominions or rulers or authorities—all things have been created through Him and for Him. He is before all things, and by Him all things hold together. (Col 1:15-17, CSB)

As it was for Isaiah, Daniel, and the Apostle John, to encounter Christ is to experience Someone *more* than we were ready for. The Scriptures seek to describe the One who is beyond words: magnificent, marvelous, wonderful, majestic, beautiful, awesome, glorious, mighty, holy, compassionate.... The more we consider and contemplate him, the bigger he gets. The Triune God is completely Other, beyond all our understanding, even beyond the standards and dimensions by which we try to understand. We live out our existence within the parameters of time and space; the same is not true for Christ. How can we, finite and temporal, ever comprehend that which is infinitely beyond our reach? To contemplate and to gaze upon him can never lead to concepts and principles by which we will understand who this beautiful One really is. Rather, the goal of our contemplation is not comprehension but wonder. Gregory of Nyssa offered this warning:

> "Every concept formed by the intellect in an attempt
> to comprehend and circumscribe the divine nature
> can succeed only in fashioning an idol, not in
> making God known."[13]

If our search to understand God cannot be the product of our thinking, then perhaps it must be the result of experiencing Christ in our hearts and spirits.

When Jesus came to earth, he embraced the finiteness of our humanity, yet without leaving the limitlessness and eternity of his divinity. Father John Behr states this clearly:

> "To put it in a very precise nutshell, just stop
> and think about this: we say repeatedly in our
> hymnography, 'Jesus Christ was born outside of time
> from the Father, inside of time from the mother.'" [14]

He did not so much come announcing a future reality as he did the invasion of something new, yet timeless: the Kingdom of heaven. Jesus walked and moved among the people of first century Palestine fully as one of them, and yet … He also lived beyond time, space, and matter as they understood them. In fact, he was Lord over them. Within the Jews' familiar paradigms, Jesus declared a bigger view of who he was.

---

13   Cited in Olivier Clement, *Roots of Christian Mysticism*, (New City Press, 2nd Ed. 1995) p.27

14   John Behr, *Journal of Religion, Peace and Justice*. Dec 30, 2017

Sabbath-time and Christ-time

The focal point of the Jews' understanding of time was Sabbath. It was a weekly reminder and decision to obey, trust, and rely on God more than their own efforts. It was a day of rest and rejuvenation. Beyond this, the Sabbath pointed to the ultimate fulfillment of God's great promises to his people: the restoration of all things to his original intention. Sabbath celebrated that a time of completion, wholeness and abundant life—Shalom—was coming. Although by Jesus' day Sabbath had taken on a rigid, often legalistic expression, its original purpose was to celebrate life.

Jesus' first words recorded in the Gospels were, "the Kingdom of God is here; repent and believe." (Mark 1:15) In Luke's account, after describing the new reality of the Kingdom, he concluded with, "Today this scripture is fulfilled." (4:21) A new time had come. For the next three years he sought to shift the Jews' focus from Sabbath-time to Christ-time. Again and again, Jesus went out of his way to engage in Kingdom activity on the Sabbath, bringing the wholeness of Shalom to the world around him. Week after week Jesus healed on the Sabbath, confronting the rigid restriction of religion and contrasting it with the abundant life that dwelt within him. A blind man receives his sight; a man with a withered hand is restored in the midst of a synagogue service; a paralytic is instantly healed; a demoniac is set free (again during a synagogue service). All of these took place on various Sabbaths. The religious leaders did not deny the authenticity of the healings; however, they didn't understand why Jesus wouldn't choose to heal on the other six days of the week instead.

Jesus was declaring a message through demonstration: "The time you have been waiting so long for is now here. This is the time of restoration, wholeness, and abundant life. God-time is no longer a special day of the week; I am God-time. I am Sabbath." Jesus made this clear when he said, "The Sabbath was made for man, not man for the Sabbath. Therefore the Son of Man is also Lord of the Sabbath." (Mk 2:27-28)

The Eternal I AM

The Apostle John emphasized the timelessness and eternity of Christ throughout his Gospel, in fact from its first words: "In the beginning was the Word and the Word was with God and the Word was God." John was making clear to his readers that God the Father and his Son, Jesus Christ, were eternally inseparable. That is why Jesus said, "If you have seen me, you have seen the Father."(-John 14:9) For the Jews, God's most holy name (which for them was not to be spoken aloud) was I AM. This was the name that God revealed to Moses at the burning bush. Therefore, the significance of John using the phrase "I am" twenty-four times in his Gospel cannot be overstated. Perhaps nowhere is this clearer than in chapter eight where Jesus explicitly says, "Before Abraham was, I AM." Jesus was challenging the Jews to think in a new way about him. Not only did his answer indicate that he was with Abraham all those centuries earlier; his "I AM" suggests that he is living in the present tense with Abraham right at that moment. Jesus lives both inside and outside of time. Obviously, the implications of this lead us to consider a great mystery.

To limit Jesus to the historical Gospel account that he came from heaven, lived among us for 33 years, then returned to heaven reflects a very small, time-and-space bound view of Christ. Scripture calls us to a greater view of Christ:

1. Christ the Son existed before creation:
"In the beginning was the Word" (Jn 1:1; and see Heb 1:2-3; Jn 8:58)

2. He dwelt in heaven with the Father:
"So now, Father, glorify me in your own presence with the glory that I had in your presence before the world existed." (Jn 17:5; and see Jn 3:31; 6:23; 1 Cor 15:47; 1 Ti 3:16)

3. He was sent from outside our world:
"God's love was revealed among us in this way: God sent his only Son into the world so that we might live through him." (1Jn 4:9; and see Lu 12:49-51; Jn 3:17; Gal 4:4; 2 Tim 1:15)

The beginning point of any pursuit of the mystery of Christ must be that Jesus Christ *is* God. We must always come back to this, because it is the foundation of everything. Jesus is not a representative, a reflection, or any other lesser view that we may have of him. The Trinity is not a pantheon with God the Father at the top and the Son and Holy Spirit positioned slightly lower. Therefore the most lofty thoughts that we can ever think about God are exactly what we must think about Jesus Christ.

Christ Beyond Time

St. Augustine once wrote that if we understand God, then he isn't God. In our own time, David Jeremiah wrote that a God who is small enough to be understood isn't big enough to be worshiped. Perhaps it is when we begin to contemplate Christ's relationship to time that we are most confronted with mystery.

What is Christ's relationship to time? Jesus Christ told John that he was the Alpha and Omega, beginning and end. Around the globe, in the Nicene Creed, believers declare: "We believe in one Lord, Jesus Christ, the only Son of God, eternally begotten of the Father." His being is eternal, stretching back before the beginning of time and endlessly forward beyond it. Simple words to read and write, but their implication is huge. Does this mean that Jesus Christ exists in every moment at all times? Does he live within all time or outside of it? Is Christ in everything as eternally "now"?

Philosophers have wrestled with this issue for centuries. On the issue of God and time, they tend to come down in one of two places:

Some believe that God is temporal, that is, he experiences some events before he experiences other events. Therefore his dealings in creation exist in the present, just as he existed in all past moments and will in all future ones. He answers our prayers in the present. The second somewhat more dominant view is that God is timeless, not existing in any one specific time. He is beyond time. This means that he experiences the past and future as a timeless "now." God does not experience and move in the tenth century before he experiences our century; for God, everything is simultaneous. Although we read about Biblical events as being in the past, as they certainly are for us, God experiences them right now *and* in the past. This view of God suggests that he is a being whose life is too full to exist only at one moment in time.[15]

Sacramental Time

Among theologians and philosophers, time itself is viewed as either univocal (having only one meaning, plain and distinct) or sacramental, meaning that past, present and future can coincide. Unlike the first 1400 years of the church, which understood time sacramentally, in our day we see time in a linear manner; however, Scripture appears to point to the reality of sacramental time. During the Transfiguration, Moses and Elijah appear with Jesus:

> "Transfiguration folds time, brings disparate events together, for this is not just a real moment between Moses, Elijah and Jesus, and between the disciples and the triune Love; it's not just this actual historic moment on Tabor where a resurrected humanity communes with the divine life. This moment also reveals the encounter with Moses and the triune Love on Sinai, and later on Sinai, Elijah's encounter with the one God, who is not present in the earthquake or the fire or the mighty wind but in a still small voice."[16]

---

15 Gregory E. Ganssle, *Internet Encyclopedia of Philosophy*, (Yale University)

16 Kenneth Tanner, *Transfiguration and the Defeat of Death*, (Clarion Journal) Feb. 14, 2021

As we have seen, "mystery" is an eternal truth that only God can reveal in his time and way; it is not something that we can figure out. In the sacrament of the Lord's Supper, we participate beyond time with what Hebrews calls the "cloud of witnesses." We are participating with what is eternally going on in the Upper Room; we are participating with the church in all ages. St. Augustine's understanding of time was sacramental: "time *participates* in the eternity of God's life, and it is this participation that is able to gather past, present, and future together in one."[17]

We live within the dimensions of time and space. We are present in one place but not another; we experience each moment sequentially, in a linear way. We see an event that took place some years ago as unrelated to what is happening today. I am not referring to cause and effect, but rather the connecting presence of Christ in those events. God is outside of time—"before Abraham was, *I AM.*" Jesus exists as much in this moment as he does in the days of the patriarchs, or looking forward, as he does at the moment he ultimately returns. A number of writers have posited a helpful picture. If time is a river, we live on the banks of that river and can therefore only see from a fixed perspective. However, God sees and experiences that same river from many thousands of feet up. Therefore he sees what has flowed past, what is currently flowing, and what will flow, all from the same perspective. This picture has limitations. It tends to present God as distant

---

17 Hans Boersma, *Heavenly Participation*, (Wm. B. Eerdmans Pub. Co. 2011) p.126

enough to see everything at once, but actually God is also personally experiencing all parts of the river at once. God not only transcends time, he embraces every detail of it. Jeremiah tells us "His compassions fail not." He continues to feel and move in compassion *continuously* in every moment of time. Nothing is ever behind him, in his past. Perhaps this is why, when confronting the Pharisees, Jesus said, "Where I am you cannot come." If I think in a linear way, this is very curious. Since he was speaking in the present about a future event, surely "where I am going" would be more appropriate. But Jesus is challenging more than their religion; he is challenging their limited paradigm.

His Mercy Endures for How Long?

To see Christ outside of time raises important questions. If, as he so clearly said, "I am in Him and He is in Me," then how does his timelessness affect me? What is the true nature of my existence? Zeph 3:17 declares that he rejoices over me with singing. This expresses a wild exuberance, literally, "He spins about wildly." Jesus continually rejoices in my past in his eternal present. While I may remember with fondness a pleasurable event, Christ is experiencing it eternally right now, without end. When I consider the past joy that my sons' births gave me, how indescribably happy I was, this leads me to a very real awareness of how Christ is experiencing me right now. I suspect that I am being given a minute glimpse into his present experience of my life. I remember with fondness; he experiences with present joy. In my moments of great pain Jesus is there. Not just that he *was* there; he *is* there right now, living that moment with me with present compassion, present intimate love. In contrast, the closest I can get to an event in my life, no matter how significant, is through my memory of it. No wonder St. Augustine wrote that "He is closer to me than I am to myself."

When I take time to consider the eternal, unchanging Christ, who lives in a state of unwavering "foreverness," and who is the Creator of the cosmos, yet not contained by his creation; then not only does wonder rise up, but also a deep, deep security. Throughout the Scriptures, which I am convinced reveal his true nature, there is a repeating refrain, like a quiet but persistent heartbeat: *His mercy endures forever; His mercy endures forever; His mercy endures forever.*

Forever. Therefore, if it is without end, then nothing can stop his mercy. Nothing I could ever do, no place I could ever go. Nothing that ever happens to me. This means that even my death cannot stop his enduring mercy toward me. "If I make my bed in Sheol, you are there." So why would I believe that his mercy has any limits? What if Paul really meant what he wrote to the Roman believers:

> *For I am convinced that neither death, nor life, nor angels, nor rulers, nor things present, nor things to come, nor powers, nor height, nor depth, nor anything else in all creation will be able to separate us from the love of God in Christ Jesus our Lord. (Ro 8:38-39)*

Christ beyond time. Christ with me and loving me forever.

Christ and Temple-Space

Just as Sabbath was holy time for the Jews, the Jerusalem Temple was holy space. This understanding went far beyond our concept of a church as the "house of the Lord." More than a place to worship God, the Temple was the intersection point of heaven and earth where both realities overlapped. This went back to the time of the tabernacle where, within the holy of holies, was the Ark of the Covenant. God's glory, his manifest presence dwelt there.

Jesus confronted the Jewish leaders over their promotion of the Temple court as a place to buy and sell for profit, instead of its true purpose of making room for "outsiders." When he overturned the money changers' tables and drove out the animals, the Jews challenged him. He responded, "Destroy this temple, and in three days I will raise it up." (Jn 2:19) This was so offensive to the Jews that it became their primary accusation against Jesus at his trial. Not only was the Temple the intersection point of heaven and earth, it brought a sense of history and social stability to a people who constantly lived with the uncertainty of being an occupied nation. If the Jews could not be sure that the Temple would stand beyond their lifetimes, what could they be sure of? To their ears, Jesus' words were more than a challenge to their most sacred traditions, they were deeply offensive.

When Jesus said, "I tell you, something greater than the Temple is here" (Mt 12:6) he was announcing a new reality: the Kingdom of heaven was now in their midst. Jesus brought this reality with him—in fact, even more than demonstrating the Kingdom, Jesus *is* the Kingdom. He is the eternal plan, intention and reality of the

Triune God. Therefore, wherever he went, there was the Kingdom of heaven. No longer was the Temple the place of intersection; Jesus is the new Temple. Perhaps even more surprising, Paul said, "For you are the Temple of the living God." (2 Cor 6:16) He wrote this because if our lives are lived in Christ, *we* are now God's Temple. We are the holy space, the divine time that intersects with earth; because of Christ, this is our true identity. We carry with us everywhere the fragrance of Christ. This is the new reality, one that we are called to live out.

It is interesting that those places in which there is a long history of worshiping Christ become sacred places where his presence can be felt and experienced. More than merely tradition or reputation is behind what draws men and women to ancient churches and cathedrals. Through centuries of adoration, Christ's presence somehow saturates the atmosphere. Whether pilgrims, visitors or worshipers have language for what they sense or not, at a deep level they are aware they have entered sacred space. This is also true at a personal level when over time, we develop a secret history with the Lord. A room, a chair, a corner of the garden can become a place of his presence, a sacred space, our own temple.

Experiencing Christ Beyond Limits

There was a day when I experienced first hand the reality of Christ beyond time and space, when "the Word became flesh." We were driving from Vancouver, Canada to the Seattle airport on our way to a meeting near Los Angeles. This meeting was vitally important to our ministry and had taken a lot of time to set up. We headed down with lots of time to spare, but then encountered a huge backup at the border crossing. As the minutes ticked by, I became aware that it was going to be impossible to make our flight. By the time we cleared the border crossing, we only had 40 minutes to make a two and a half hour journey. Discouraged and upset, I told my wife that we should just turn around and go home. She countered that we should drive down anyway; perhaps the flight would be delayed. I did not drive above the speed limit because there was no point, yet we arrived at the airport with 20 minutes to spare. This was a physical impossibility. I was not aware of the scenery flashing by; I don't know if we skipped entire cities on the way. All I know is that in a matter of minutes we went 125 miles. Had our watches stopped? Did we somehow have the wrong time? No, Christ had taken us with him beyond the limitation of time (2 1/2 hours) and space (125 miles).

Contemplating the Limitless Christ

Paul makes the astonishing claim that "all this was created by him, through him, and for him." Even more, Paul tells us that Christ holds all things together (Col 1:17 NLT). No matter how unfathomably enormous the cosmos is (and it is constantly expanding), Jesus Christ embraces it within himself. He is completely *beyond* and at the same time, fully *in* all space. David contemplated this as he wrote,

> *If I ascend to heaven, you are there;*
> *if I make my bed in Sheol, you are there.*
> *If I take the wings of the morning*

and settle at the farthest limits of the sea,
even there your hand shall lead me (Ps 139:8-10a)

As David contemplated the mystery of Christ, it led him to a fresh awareness of his immanence:

For it was you who formed my inward parts;
you knit me together in my mother's womb.
I praise you, for I am fearfully and wonderfully made.
Wonderful are your works;
that I know very well.
My frame was not hidden from you,
when I was being made in secret,
intricately woven in the depths of the earth. (vv 13-15)

And here is the paradox of contemplating the greatness of Christ: as we grow in awareness of how vast he is, beyond the boundaries that we place upon him, our consciousness of him becomes more deeply intimate.

"For you possess my heart, O Lord" (v13, LXX)

Meditating upon the infinite and eternal Christ leads us to another great mystery. Paul declared that not only does Christ contain the fullness of creation, he also contains the fullness of the Trinity.

For in Him the entire fullness of God's nature dwells
bodily in Christ, and you have been filled by Him, who is
the head over every ruler and authority. (Col 2:9-10 CSB)

And still the mystery grows: we have been filled by this infinite One. And lest we miss this, Jesus said the same thing to his disciples: "I am in the Father, and you are in me, and I am in you." Christ states this as fact, not something to which we attain, but already accomplished. How can we actually live in the reality of this?

To seek after truth with the intellect is interesting, but it is the inner knowledge of the heart which transforms us. This *knowing* comes through contemplating Christ in stillness: "Be still and know that I am God." To experience him in and beyond space, we must learn to still ourselves, to find that sacred space where we can be silent. As we do, time begins to slow down, heightening our awareness of the vastness of the cosmos and that Christ embraces it all. At times, our thoughts about him begin to expand with new insights and possibilities of who he really is.[18]

Rather than feeling lost or overwhelmed at his vastness, a great peace rises up, an even greater security that the Transcendent One who mysteriously resides in me will never abandon me. He loves me; he rejoices over me; he desires me even more than I desire him. In stillness, I move between heart-waves that travel outwardly to him and inwardly from him—waves that illuminate and transfigure.

Once again, we are confronted with Paul's ecstatic prayer for the Ephesians:

> *I pray that you may have the power to comprehend, with all the saints, what is the breadth and length and height and depth, and to know the love of Christ that surpasses knowledge, so that you may be filled with all the fullness of God. (Eph 3:18-19)*

---

18   Keith Giles, (https://www.patheos.com/blogs/ keithgiles/2019/06/how_christ_transcends_all_space_and_time/)

George MacDonald described this journey:

"[A]t length the glory of our existence flashes upon us, we face full to the sun that enlightens what is sent forth, and know ourselves alive with an infinite life, even the life of the Father. Then indeed we *are*; then indeed we have life; the life of Jesus has, through light, become life in us; the glory of God in the face of Jesus mirrored in our hearts, has made us alive; we are one with God for ever and ever."[19]

Christ Beyond Matter

If Jesus Christ lives eternally beyond the confines of time and space, then surely he is not restricted by the laws of matter. When Jesus came to earth he brought the new and final reality of the Kingdom of heaven. Within this heavenly reality even matter itself changed. The physical laws are now under the dominion of the King. It is not that the physical laws are suddenly void; rather, it is that at any given moment the reality of heaven can break into our world. At a word, fish jump into nets; a decomposing body comes back to life; food is multiplied to feed thousands; a storm instantly stops and waves disappear. In fact, the very physics of water changes: it becomes solid enough to walk on; instantly it is transformed to wine. All of these signs reveal an unrestricted Christ.

I grew up in a time when much of the church, rather than letting these miracles reveal the greatness of Christ,

---

19   George MacDonald, *Creation in Christ*, (Regent College Publishing, 1976) p.27

instead tried to explain them away in naturalist terms. The Red Sea was only a few feet deep. (Then how did an entire Egyptian army drown in it?) Jesus didn't multiply the loaves and fish; he set an example of the power of sharing. This is because our natural man, what Paul calls the flesh, is afraid of new ways of thinking, preferring to cling to old paradigms. It has always been thus.

When Christ's Kingdom Breaks In

The first time I saw the Lord multiply food was at a church gathering at a community center about twenty years ago. We had planned a small "agape feast" for 70 people. There were 72 pork buns prepared and counted out. Likewise, various large salads and other food were prepared with seventy people in mind. However, someone misunderstood and thought the meal was for the neighborhood and invited all the neighbors to join us. And they came. And came. Several church members approached me and suggested that we take up a quick collection to go and buy more food. But my wife (again) said, "Let's just wait and see what the Lord does." Not only was our gathering now twice the anticipated size, I couldn't help but notice that many of our guests were taking two or even three pork buns and piling their plates high. After everyone had eaten, my wife and I lined up. There were still two buns left; there were two servings of fruit salad; in fact, there were two helpings of everything. How did Jesus do it? Like the trip to Seattle, I don't know. It is just that the food never ran out.

That was the first of a number of similar episodes over the past twenty years. I have watched him move beyond the laws of matter to multiply food for the hungry, and medicine, in the Philippines, Zambia, Uganda, Tanzania, and Kenya. On one occasion, we finished a day of medical clinics with only 70 doses of an important anti-parasite left. We announced that the tablets would be distributed outside. When we went out, we counted 472 people waiting to receive the pills. At first we thought that we dare not give away what we had, because it could cause a great disturbance. However, we decided to go ahead for as long as we had the medicine to give. By now, you may not be surprised to read that the final person received the last tablet. There seems to be an important lesson in this. If we give away what we have, like the disciples distributing a few loaves and fishes to a huge crowd, the food, or medicine, or anything else, is multiplied in the process of giving.

Does this always happen? Of course not. But occasionally, the Kingdom of heaven breaks in. King Jesus reminds us that he is bigger than we thought. He really has created and continues to hold all things in the cosmos together.

I believe that Christ's rule over matter is revealed in our physical bodies as well. When Jesus brought the Kingdom of heaven to this realm, all the possibilities changed. He carried the reality of heaven with him. That is why the blind, the deaf, the paralyzed, and the sick were healed. For over forty years I have watched him continue to heal in the same way. By his great mercy, Jesus has let me witness more healing than I could ever remember: blind eyes and deaf ears opened; limbs lengthened; the paralyzed get up and walk; cancer and HIV/AIDS instantly healed (all confirmed by medical authorities).

All of this because of who he is and the new reality that has broken into our world and is continuing to advance.

As we behold his glory, as we let our hearts be enlarged by and toward the One, beyond any limitations that we (unconsciously) place on him, we are being transformed into his likeness.

> *And all of us, with unveiled faces, seeing the glory of the Lord as though reflected in a mirror, are being transformed (transfigured) into the same image from one degree of glory to another, for this comes from the Lord, the Spirit. (2 Cor 3:18)*

Christ invites us to pursue the unsearchable riches of who he really is. And as we learn to allow him to take us on a journey both outward and inward, our paradigms are changed, our hearts and minds are stretched, and we discover and participate in a more eternally and infinitely beautiful gospel.

* * *

We live in a universe filled with mystery so profound that often we have no language with which to accurately describe it. Two particles billions of light years away move in perfect tandem; particles arrive before they are transported. When I was in school in the 1960's we were told that there were thousands of galaxies in the universe; given that there are an average of 100 billion stars in each one, this number was hard to imagine. With increasingly more powerful and accurate telescopes, the estimated number of galaxies grew to millions, then billions. Truly mind boggling. But now, the estimate is *two trillion galaxies*. How can we even fathom such a number?

On Christmas Day, 2021 the James Webb telescope was launched. I think that there is significance in that date, for on the day when Christ's birth is celebrated around the globe, a portal was opened whereby we could now see into the mysteries of the cosmos—time, space and matter—at a level greatly beyond what we have ever been able to observe before. Indescribable beauty. "The heavens declare your glory" is daily taking on ever-increasing meaning, beyond what most of us have ever imagined.

As the Webb telescope sends back images of solar systems, galaxies, and black holes, we are witnessing not only unfathomable distances, but also we are peering into time from the deepest past. So far, it has projected astonishing images to earth that were created thirteen billion years ago. Currently, astrophysicists' best estimate of the origins of the universe is 13.7 billion years. For those who are committed to a young earth (about six thousand years old), it seems to me that there is no true point of contention. Scripture tells us that with God a thousand years is as a day. He has never been contained within our time-frame, and I suspect that our understanding of the universe's age, whether young or old, is not very important to him.

What happened billions of years ago, we are now experiencing as present celestial activity. This is hard to get our minds around. Surely this points to Christ living in the eternal now, beyond the confines where we work out our lives. For years when counseling those who have experienced great trauma, I encouraged them to go back to that incident and picture Jesus being with them. However, my journey into the mystery of Christ has led me to truly experience him—may I say literally and tangibly—as present in the pain of the moment, and always present *in that moment.*

The New Testament writers tell us that we are joined with the great cloud of witnesses, those who we think of as having gone before us in the past. Hebrews tells us that we have come to the church of the firstborn—that we are right now with Peter and John; with the Church Fathers; with Wesley, Spurgeon and a host of others—not just that we will be with them when we get to heaven; we are with them right now. So as I read about Abraham, David, and Isaiah I am not just remembering them; in the eternal reality that we share in Christ I am *with* them. This has greatly changed how I read the Gospels. I am not remembering what Jesus did and experienced so much as I am with him. Third person past (Jesus healed the blind man) has become second person present (You are healing that man right now, and I am here with You).

For several years, praying the Nicene Creed has been a part of my personal time with Christ. I attend a liturgical church where together we recite this every week. I greatly value this corporate practice as it expresses both the doctrine and mystery that required over two hundred years to craft (second to fourth century). But even beyond this, my participation takes me beyond my own time-space limitations. As we in our congregation pray the sacred words of the Nicene Creed, we are joining with others across seventeen hundred years. And beyond our own personal space, we are joining with over a billion other Christ-followers from around the globe.

To Him who is, and was, and ever shall be.

"Forever – is composed of Nows –
'Tis not a different time –
Except for Infiniteness –
And Latitude of Home"
(Emily Dickinson)

CHAPTER TWO

Christ in Creation

My journey of pursuing Christ has been full of surprises. One of those has been a steadily growing awareness of, and love for, the natural world. I am now seeing and hearing what for decades I was blind and deaf to. As Jesus becomes more beautiful to me, so does his creation. Indeed, this should not have been a surprise since both Creator and creation are intrinsically connected, each revealing truths about the other. William Wordsworth, a Christian, captured this synergy in much of his poetry:

> "It is a beauteous evening, calm and free,
> The holy time is quiet as a Nun
> Breathless with adoration; the broad sun
> Is sinking down in its tranquility;
> The gentleness of heaven broods o'er the Sea;
> Listen! the mighty Being is awake,
> And doth with his eternal motion make"
>
> (It Is A Beauteous Evening, 1802)

Perhaps the best way to consider Christ in creation is to look before creation, when there was nothing material. God did not take anything that already existed and shape it into creation. As humans, we can build from existing materials, but we cannot create. Only God can do that. The term for what God began with before creation is *ex nihilo*—out of nothing. "He calls into existence the things that do not exist." (Ro 4:17)

Christ then created something that was totally outside himself, and in doing so, he made room for it in his Being. It is vitally important to hold onto the truth that what he created was *of* himself—God created out of the unwavering love that is his essence, and that divine love is therefore in everything. For the first time, there was something that was "other." This did not happen randomly. From the beginning (actually, before the beginning), creation was an act of will and not chance. This is the foundation of all time, space, and matter. This is the foundation on which creation, including you and me, always stands.

Christ beyond time, space and matter—and then … everything begins with what may be the most well known verse in the Bible:

In the beginning, God created the heavens and the earth.

From *ex nihilo* to beginning. From eternal only, to eternal *and.*

> "[Creation] is a work of the will, and is thus not co-eternal with God. For it is not possible that which is brought from not-being into being should be co-eternal with that which exists always and without origin."[20]

---

20   Vladimir Lossky citing St John Damascene, *The Mystical Theology of the Eastern Church,* (St. Vladimir's Seminary Press, 1976) p.93

Creation begins and therefore springs from non-being into being. Thus change enters time and space. As St. Gregory of Nyssa wrote, "It [creation] begins to be, and the very substance of the creation owes its beginning to change." As we consider Christ in creation, we must hold onto two truths: first, creation was, is, and always will be an act of God's will and not chance. Second, within the dimensions of time and space, creation is continually in a state of *becoming*. Creation is changing, in motion, moving toward its final fulfillment: to both reflect and exist within the perfection of the Triune God.

The first thought that comes to mind when we read *beginning* is that it simply means the start of something, and clearly that is contained within the word which in Hebrew is *reishit*, and in Greek is *arche*. However, a closer examination reveals a greater richness, especially as we consider the role of Christ in creation.

Strong's defines *reishit* as the first, in place, time, order or rank (specifically a firstfruit; beginning, the chief, principal thing). *Reishit* means "beginning" but also "origin," "source" and "firstly." In the Greek OT, the Septuagint, "beginning" is translated as *arche*. Besides meaning that which comes first it carries a broader meaning: the original source. *Arche* is that by which everything begins to be; for example, the English word archetype signifies "the original type."

As we have seen, Christ lives both beyond time and within it. He appeared at "just the right time" (Gal 4:4). He gives us time as a gift, and within that gift, he teaches us to live actively in the present moment, not obsessing over past hurts and failures, nor worrying about the future. "Today" is his gift to us.

> "Creation is nothing but the time God has made for us, and salvation is his work of harmonizing past and present and future, and drawing us into the rhythms of his own life."[21]

The Word Speaks

The New Testament repeatedly identifies Christ as that original source, the Father's agent in creation. Hebrews 1:3 tells us, "He is the reflection of God's glory and the exact imprint of God's very being, and he sustains all things by his powerful word." In verse 10 we see Ps 102:25 applied to Christ:

> *Long ago you laid the foundation of the earth,*
> *and the heavens are the work of your hands. (CSB)*

Christ is the Logos—the Word—and, of course the Word *speaks*. He spoke creation into being:

> *By the word of the Lord the heavens were made*
> *and all their host by the breath of his mouth ...*
> *let all the inhabitants of the world stand in awe of him,*
> *for he spoke, and it came to be;*
> *he commanded, and it stood firm. (Ps 33:6,8,9)*

His first creative words were, "Let there be light." As we begin to see Christ beyond the bounds of time, a more

---

21 Chris E.W. Green, *All Things Beautiful*, (Baker University Press, 2021) p.26

eternal significance comes into focus when Jesus says, "I am the light of the world." John was very intentional in referring to light sixteen times in his Gospel. As we consider that the second Person of the Godhead is the "light of the world," Jesus' words lead us beyond knowing that he is a beacon of light to his primordial presence throughout all of creation.

The Apostle John insists that Jesus Christ is the Son of God, coequal and of the same substance with the Father. This is the central truth upon which John declares his Gospel:

In the beginning was the Word (Logos), and the Word was with God, and the Word was God ... All things came into being through him, and without him not one thing came into being. (Jn 1:1,3)

John intentionally used *Logos* to describe Jesus Christ. Although translated as "Word," it carries multiple meanings and connotations, including: mind, rational order, expression, manifestation, revelation, and original principle.[22]

The Apostle Paul tells us that all of the cosmos was made by and for Christ the Word. Jesus stands at the center of time, space, and the entire universe. He is the single connecting point: He created and is creating all of the cosmos, and in turn, every aspect of the cosmos is being transformed and will find its ultimate end and purpose in him. Contemplating this boggles the mind.

---

22 David Bentley Hart, *The New Testament,* (Yale University Press 2017) p.550

Creation, the Trinity, and Me

According to John's Gospel, Christ, the Logos, was both with God and was God Himself. This helps us to understand the Trinitarian mystery of creation: it was ordained by the Father, spoken into being by the Son and is sustained by the Holy Spirit. Whatever is created by the Father receives its existence by the Word (the Son). This is why St. Irenaeus described the Son and the Holy Spirit as the two hands of God. He wrote,

> "As God is verbal, therefore He made created things by the Word; and God is Spirit, so that He adorned all things by His Spirit ... Thus, since the Word 'establishes,' that is, works bodily and confers existence, while the Spirit arranges and forms the various 'powers,' so rightly is the Son called Word and the Spirit the Wisdom of God."[23]

Creation, including you and me, is the expression of the eternally joyful activity of the Father, Son and Holy Spirit. The Father is the origin or cause of creation. The Son reveals and activates that cause. The Holy Spirit is the life-giving breath of God who "is causing each thing and the universe as a whole to tend in the direction of that purpose."[24] The early church fathers described this activity of the Trinity as the divine dance, in Greek, *perichoresis*, from which we get the word "choreography." A dance seems to be the best way to capture the ever-chang-

---

23 St. Irenaeus, *On the Apostolic Preaching*, translated by John Behr, (St. Vladimir's Seminary Press, 1997) p.43

24 Olivier Clement, *Roots of Christian Mysticism*, (New City Press, 2nd Ed. 1995) p.27

ing, joyful, participatory, celebratory activity of the Trinity. It is Trinity that makes creation good. *Perichoresis* is the fellowship of three co-equal Persons perfectly embraced in love and harmony and expressing an intimacy that no one can humanly comprehend. God created out of the abundance and overflow of what he eternally experiences within himself. What we are invited to experience in creation is the overflow of his perichoretic life.

> *Let the heavens be glad, and let the earth rejoice;*
> *let the sea roar, and all that fills it;*
> *let the field exult, and everything in it.*
> *Then shall all the trees of the forest sing for joy*
> *before the LORD (Ps 96:11-13)*

The most famous artistic depiction of the Triune God is an icon painted by Andrei Rublev in the fifteenth century, entitled *The Trinity* (or *The Hospitality of Abraham*). It presents each of the three Persons sitting in a circle, but it is a circle that is open to the viewer, inviting him or her in. As Jesus said, "I am in the Father, and you are in me, and I am in you." (Jn14:20) The Triune community is the source from which all creation derives its value because it is a reflection and expression of the infinite value that the Three Persons find in each other. The Triune God is love *within* himself and *toward* us and all creation.

In the opening phrase of the Bible an inseparable link is established between creation and the Creator. Each reveals the other. Just as a painting is first conceived within the heart and mind of the artist and therefore that painting reveals something about the artist, so creation reveals the heart of God. Creation is not God; that is pantheism. However, creation is contained *within* God (panentheism).The Wisdom of Solomon states, "Your immortal Spirit is in all things." (12:1) Accordingly, while creation is "other," it is not separate from God. Creation is not to be worshiped, but it is to be embraced as a reflection of who God is and therefore a means by which he reveals himself. Contrary to projections of an angry or disappointed God who sits in judgment, from the beginning of time, his unfailing and unchanging word over his creation remains: "And God saw that it was good." God's creation was willed by him, he declared it good, and for all eternity it will be the object of his delight and joy.

From the moment that God said "Let there be," change became part of reality. However, that change will not, indeed cannot, mean the end of creation, but rather is moving toward one that is perfected. It was spoken into being by the Eternal One, and that word was spoken for all time.

Yes, the world is established; it shall never be moved.
(Ps 93:1 ESV)

Christ the Word has spoken and that creative word will never cease.

The 'Divine Dance' of the Trinity never stops; and therefore Christ never ceases from his creative activity. One of the great miracles of the Cross is that we have been invited into that Dance. When we make room in our hearts and imaginations to express ourselves in original ways, more than "letting the creative juices flow," we align ourselves with the activity of our Creator God. Often, in the midst of writing, painting or composing, we discover something rising up, an awakening from deep inside. This creative process is not entirely earthly; we are also drawing upon the reality of heaven. In creating, we are synchronizing our minds, hearts and spirits with God's creative force. This creativity is actualized beyond the arts, whether in business or the kitchen, the counseling office or the garden. However creatively expressed, when we dare to believe that we are resonating with his divine, creative flow, there are times when we know Christ and ourselves, with a clarity that unites our hearts with his, with heaven and earth, and with the ancient and the new.

> *So shall My word be that goes forth from My mouth;*
> *It shall not return to Me void,*
> *But it shall accomplish what I please,*
> *And it shall prosper in the thing for which I sent it.*
> *(Is 55:11 NKJV)*

Creation and the Cross

Christ declares, "I am the Alpha and the Omega, the first and the last, the beginning and the end." He encompasses time. At both the beginning and the end, he *is*. Once again, John uses the word *arche*, rather than the more typical *protos*. Christ is certainly the original source of creation, the One who spoke it into being. But in his declaration to be the end, we can see another aspect of his ongoing creative work. Beyond bracketing time, Jesus is telling us that he is not only the source of creation; He is creation's *goal*. "He will live with them. They will be His people,

and God himself will be with them and be their God."
(Revelation 21:3, ESV)

Maximus the Confessor wrote,

> "Christ is the great hidden mystery, the blessed goal,
> the purpose for which everything was created ...
> With his gaze fixed on this goal God called things
> into existence ... He is the mystery which surrounds
> all ages. In fact it is for the sake of Christ, and for
> his mystery that all ages exist and all that they
> contain."[25]

Maximus is expressing a deep mystery. The essence
of salvation is to reflect the perfection of Christ; therefore,
creation and the saving glory of God revealed at the Cross
are directly connected. The power of the Cross was and is
the same power exhibited in creation.

> "We do not speak of a power in the Cross that is
> different from that through which the worlds came
> into being, a power which is eternal and without
> beginning and which guides creation all the time
> without any break, in a divine way and beyond the
> understanding of all, in accordance with the will of
> his divinity."[26]

In his Incarnation, Passion and crucifixion, Christ
emptied himself, as Paul wrote:

---

25 Maximus the Confessor, cited by Olivier Clement, *The Roots of
    Christian Mysticism*, p.39

26 St. Isaac the Syrian, cited by John Behr, *The Mystery of Christ*, (St.
    Vladimir's Seminary Press 2006) p.90

Instead, he emptied himself,
and received the form of a slave,
being born in the likeness of humans.
And then, having human appearance,
he humbled himself, and became
obedient even to death,
yes, even the death of the cross. (Phil 2:7-8)

Taking on human likeness and fully identifying with the human condition meant Christ emptying himself—*kenosis*. According to this passage, this emptying began at his Incarnation, and reached its climax at the Cross. We will look at this in more depth later, but *kenosis* does not mean that Christ set aside his divinity; kenotic love is actually an expression of his divinity. The Incarnation did not make him somehow less or in any way separate from the Father; fully God, Jesus Christ took on the full existence of Man. In one sense, he was now even *more*. That the limitless One could become more is a mystery beyond our comprehension. If this is the case, then in what way was Christ emptied? He set aside, not his divine nature, but his divine privilege. It was his divinity that qualified Jesus to redeem the world through his suffering and death.

The Triune God was and is infinitely and eternally complete in himself. Just as Christ emptied himself without becoming less, in creation, the Trinity emptied itself of sole Being. God is the Original Cause, still the Eternal One, but now there is "Other" because now there is God *and* something else—creation. One of the great Russian theologians of the 20th century, Sergius Bulgakov, points out that creation can never be left outside the purposes and providence of God, which is the image of God's love for creation. From the beginning of time, the Triune God has been at work in his creation, helping it to become its true self, instilling in it all the fullness of the Godhead.[27] Creation and the Cross are eternally linked because what Christ spoke into being—the shared life of God and his creation—was most clearly demonstrated in the union of God and Man at the Incarnation, and will reach its fulfillment at his Second Coming when he will make *all things* new. Creation is embraced by God, but it is not God.

With his word, Christ created something that he declared was good. But more than this, he created the cosmos with a purpose: to move toward its great calling to be perfectly united with him. This is creation's calling and unshakable destiny. The reconciling power of the Cross reaches even beyond our human lives to all of the universe.

Paul understood this mystery and so wrote,

> *For the creation eagerly waits with anticipation for God's sons to be revealed. For the creation was subjected to futility—not willingly, but because of him who subjected it—in the hope that the creation itself will also be set free from the bondage to decay into the glorious freedom of God's children. For we know that the whole creation has been groaning together with labor pains until now. (Ro 8:19-22 CSB)*

---

27 Sergius Bulgakov, *Judas Iscariot*, np

We humans are unique among creation; we are created "a little lower than the angels." Perhaps in some way the condition of the universe is connected to our own. That is why creation is waiting for our true selves to be revealed as sons and daughters of God in Christ. This is why the Cross, the axis of everything—time, space, matter—is connected right now to creation, reconciling it to himself.

> *For God was pleased to have*
> *all his fullness dwell in him,*
> *and through him to reconcile*
> *everything to himself,*
> *whether things on earth or things in heaven,*
> *by making peace*
> *through his blood, shed on the cross. (Col 1:19-20 CSB)*

Two Watershed Doctrines

Ex Nihilo

The mystery of Christ in creation is, as Paul wrote, *unsearchable, unfathomable*. Christ spoke the planets, stars, galaxies—too many and too beautiful to fully comprehend—into being. And he did it all from nothing (*ex nihilo*) outside of himself. And because he was the originator of all that was created, therefore it was a beautiful, perfect creation, something to be cherished. Among early Christians and Fathers, this was foundational. God always *was*, and therefore, creation came from him, and followed him. The point of *ex nihilo* is that God is the Original Source; apart from him there is not, nor was there ever, anything.

However, over time an aspect of this truth became distorted. Beginning in the third century, then flourishing under the influence of the emperor Constantine, when Christianity became the official religion of the Empire, the doctrine of *ex nihilo* became a major colonizing influence. Now the Roman Empire, embracing this doctrine, operated from the premise that the hinterlands were re-created "out of nothing," justifying them being coerced into the Roman Christian world. Because the material world was largely neutral, for the forces of Empire, *ex nihilo* became a foundation and justification for persecuting, forced colonizing, and evangelizing other peoples for the benefit of the one true Empire and Church.[28]

By overlooking its sacred origin, that the Creator's divinity saturated every atom of the cosmos, the western church lost its awareness of creation's direct connection with the Creator. This served the Empire well; if creation is neutral, then the life of my enemy is not sacred. In our day, this has not changed in our attitudes toward enemy nations, and creation itself. A neutral world can be used solely for our selfish and short-sighted aims. The vital distinction is that creation was born out of the substance of God, *not* out of nothing. Therefore, all of creation is sacred. The implications of this distortion have been devastating from that time until this.

---

28 Taylor & Francis Group, (https://www.taylorfrancis.com/chapters/mono/10.4324/9780203879269-7/ex-nihilo-origin-empire-whitney-bauman?context=ubx&refId=5c2e005e-fe01-45af-84d4-ac07a748330e)

Original Sin

Like *ex nihilo*, the doctrine of original sin has had an enormous influence on both Catholic and Reformed theology over the centuries. It states that because of the sin of Adam, original innocence was lost and all subsequent human beings are born into a state of sinfulness. This was first expressed by Augustine in the early fifth century. He based this doctrine upon a Latin translation of Rom. 5:12, "Wherefore as by one man sin entered into this world and by sin death: and so death passed upon all men, *in whom* all have sinned." Augustine concluded that all humans are "in Adam" and have sinned in him; therefore, like Adam all are in bondage to death and estrangement from God. In other words, we have automatically inherited both depravity and guilt. The doctrine of original sin is completely dependent upon Rom. 5:12; unfortunately, this doctrine is based upon a poor Latin translation of the original Greek (Augustine did not read Greek). The NRSV is an accurate translation: "Therefore, just as sin came into the world through one man, and death came through sin, and so death spread to all *because* all have sinned." All have sinned, but it was *our* sin, not Adam's.

The consequences of the doctrine of original sin are momentous. It declares that, rather than being born in the image of God, we are born depraved and fallen; therefore, we are born separated from God, and destined for wrath and punishment. If God is angry toward us, it follows that Jesus became our protector from God's wrath. It is interesting that, like the doctrine of *ex nihilo*, for the church of Empire, which was emerging in Augustine's time, original sin was an excellent means to control people through the fear of God's anger. (Sadly, this is still true in churches today. I once heard a pastor express that if there was no fear of God's wrath and hell, why would anyone become a Christian? Jesus came to give us abundant life, not protection from the judgment of an angry God.)

While no one should deny the reality of ancestral sin and its devastating impact upon human history, this is not the same as original sin. We are not born inherently sinful or bad. Rather, we bear the image of God, but through our own sins that image is marred. And what is that image? It is the very nature of God—*Imago Dei*—that both forms us and, in the core of our being, indwells us. We are formed by the love of God which we all share with him from the beginning of creation. This is the critical issue, affecting our theology, our view of humanity, and therefore our practice. Either we see people as depraved, sinful clones of Adam, destined for wrath and punishment, *or* we see them as beloved by God yet vulnerable to the same failures and self-will of Adam.[29] Our sin is not who we are, but a denial of our created human goodness.

In the Incarnation, Christ came as fully God and fully Man; he shares our humanity and therefore shows us what it means to be truly human. This Man was sinless. His life demonstrated our true identity, hidden in him. His death defeated forever the power of sin to control us. This is critical for all believers: the sinlessness of Christ is *greater and more powerful* than the collective sin of humanity.

> *For if by the one man's trespass the many died, how*
> *much more have the grace of God and the gift overflowed*

---

29 Brad Jersak, https://bradjersak.com, Oct. 19, 2020

to the many by the grace of the one man, Jesus Christ.
(Ro 5:15, CSB)

Because of this, we have the capacity to participate, not in original sin, but original goodness. We are wounded by sin, but our identity is not defined by it. "Sin does not define us; Christ does that."[30]

The Sacredness of Creation

Most of us think of creation in a static sense; it is something that Christ did, marvelous beyond our understanding, but something in the deep past. However, if Jesus Christ is the same yesterday, today, and forever, and if his creation is the expression of himself, then perhaps we need to think in a more dynamic way. Not that he *did* create; he is the Creator *right now*. He is creating today and will continue to create forever. Paul wrote that Christ not only created everything in both the visible and invisible realm, he continues to be at work, holding all things together (Col 1:16-17). We now know that the universe is always expanding, accelerating as it does so. This is the dynamic work of Christ. Remember, beginning by its very nature means change.

To think of the act of creation as something that Christ did in the distant past, is to hold it as a memorial in our hearts. To see him at work actively right now, continuously creating, is to see the cosmos as an altar, a present place to worship him. In Genesis 15, Christ called Abraham out of his tent one night to look at the stars, promising

---

30 Kenneth Tanner, www.voicesinmyheadpodcast.com

Abraham that his descendants would be as numerous as what he was seeing. This scene captures the wonder that most of us have experienced looking up in the night sky, aware of our smallness and God's vastness. (I once heard someone say that the saddest thing about being an atheist was not having anyone to thank when looking at the stars.)

> *The heavens declare the glory of God; the skies proclaim the work of his hands. (Ps 19:1, NIV)*

Because Christ's divine creativity is always present, creation itself interacts with me as a *theophany*, as a true expression of who he is. The Son is always revealing himself through all that he has created and is creating. As the Nicene Creed declares, God created all things both seen and unseen. He created and holds both realms together. When Jesus Christ entered the world as a human, the Creator became part of his creation. He became God and man in perfect union—God Incarnate. And so the invisible One became visible. Like the Cross, the Incarnation is directly joined to creation; both happened and will continue to happen for all time.

> *In the arche, Christ created the heavens and the earth — the visible and invisible. (Gen 1:1 LXX)*

There are times when we stand in awe of Christ's majesty; gazing upon the ocean or a mountain range evokes an awareness of his transcendence, how big, how beyond us he truly is. The Psalms are filled with such expressions. When we pull aside in contemplation, time seems to slow down as we touch something of the eternal.

And in this slowing, our awareness of Christ the Creator begins to pulse inside us. Paradoxically, in the midst of his vastness, we become aware of his nearness, that in his creation he embraces us. Often this leads to seeing his reflection in the intimacy of smallness—a simple flower, bird, tree, or even a colored pebble.

For the church father Origen, Christ the Word was always actively speaking to us through both the Scriptures and creation.

> "'Lift up your eyes and see how the fields are already white for harvest.' (Jn 4:35) … The Word is in the midst of his disciples. He is asking His hearers to lift up their eyes toward the fields of the Scriptures and toward that other field where the Word is present in every creature, however small, so that they may perceive the whiteness and the brilliant radiance of the light of Truth which is everywhere."[31]

More than 1500 years ago St. Gregory Nazianzen wrote marvelous poems and hymns that celebrated creation, songs that remain fresh today. He saw the whole world as a theophany, an appearance and reflection of God.

> "No mind can grasp Thee …
> All things proclaim Thee—things that can speak,
> things that cannot.
> All things revere Thee—things that have reason,
> things that have none.
> The whole world's longing and pain mingle about

---

31 Origen, Commentary on John's Gospel. Cited in Olivier Clement, *The Roots of Christian Mysticism*, p.218

Thee.
All things breathe Thee a prayer, a silent hymn of
Thy own composing.
All that exists Thee uphold, all things in concert
move to Thy orders."

(St. Gregory Naziazen, *All-transcendent God*)

Creation is never to be worshiped, but by experiencing Christ within that which he created, we are invited into deeper communion with him. St. Augustine said that the cosmos is the first Bible. "With an awakened awareness of Christ in the midst of the world around us, we can participate in the visible and invisible praise and prayer, the eyes and ears of our hearts opened to the never-ceasing reality that everything is praying, every creature is singing the glory of God."[32] As we become conscious of the ongoing, ever-creating dynamic between Christ and his creation, inevitably a new and great appreciation, even love, for our world rises up in us.

From the beginning, in Genesis 1:26, the Lord called us to care for his creation; this is known as "the dominion mandate." This is something that we have failed to do. The results of this failure become more evident every year as the land and seas heat up. The United Nations report that currently there are almost one million species that are in danger of extinction. We are intrinsically connected to our world and we cannot avoid this truth. But if obedience to the dominion mandate that God gave us has not been strong enough to change our attitude and actions toward our world, perhaps love will be.

---

32 Olivier Clement, *The Roots of Christian Mysticism*, p.16

St. Isaac the Syrian, who lived in the seventh century, wrote with great insight and revelation about the infinite love of God. He recognized the link that Christ has with his creation. As Isaac's love for Christ deepened, so did his love for all that Christ had made. The Apostle John wrote:

Anyone who does not love his brother, whom he has seen, cannot love God, whom he has not seen. (1 Jn 4:20)

St. Isaac applied this truth to creation:

"What is a charitable heart? It is a heart that is burning with charity for the whole of creation, for men, for the birds, for the beasts, for the demons— for all creatures. He who has such a heart cannot see or call to mind a creature without his eyes becoming filled with tears by reason of the immense compassion that seizes his heart, a heart that is softened and can no longer bear to see or learn from others of any suffering, even the smallest pain, being inflicted upon a creature."[33]

Admittedly, Isaac's words seem a little intense, but they carry an important truth. God is love and therefore creation is an expression of his love, with all its seeming contradictions and perplexities. The closer our hearts get to Christ, the more we learn to abide in his love, the more we will love his creation. Love will become the foundation for caring about, and for, Creation. "In his way to union with God, man in no way leaves creatures aside, but

---

33 https://www.spiritualityandpractice.com/quotes/quotations/view/35553/spiritual-quotation

gathers together in his love the whole cosmos disordered by sin, that it may at last be transfigured by grace."[34] One of our acts of sincere love for Christ's creation is to pray for his goodness to be displayed. All of creation is groaning, as it waits for the sons and daughters of God.

* * *

For a number of years now, I have been drawn to Celtic Christianity (maybe it's because of my Scotch-Irish heritage). One of the predominant characteristics of this Church stream is how connected to the earth it is. Celtic Christians do not worship nature as God, but deeply honor how Christ expresses himself through creation. As I wrote earlier, my now lengthy journey into the mystery of Christ has opened my eyes to how, in nature, he reveals himself to me. This is a beautiful journey. The greatest of all Celtic theologians, John Scotus Eriugena, taught that Christ both reveals himself and teaches us through the Scriptures and creation. He likened this to two shoes, both of which are necessary to move forward. His studies on the Gospel of John's Prologue are filled with wonderful observations about just how much Christ reveals and cherishes all of life.

> "Consider the infinite, multiple power of the seed—
> how many grasses, fruits, and animals are contained
> in each kind of seed; and how there surges forth
> from each a beautiful, innumerable multiplicity of

---

34 Vladimir Lossky, *The Mystical Theology of the Eastern Church*, (St. Vladimir's Seminary Press 1976) p.111

forms ... From the contemplation of such as these ... illuminated and supported by divine grace ... you will see how all things made by the Word live in the Word and are life."[35]

If creation, by being formed out of nothing (*ex nihilo*) is neutral, then we can treat it (and one another) as a commodity to be used to our advantage. But surely, with the backlash of climate change striking all over the world with yet another "storm of the century" every few weeks, and with the rapid escalation of, for example, respiratory-related deaths, it is time for a radical and deep shift. Trying to preserve our way of life as a motivation for tackling climate change is clearly not working—perhaps this is because it is built upon what is good for *us*.

If I can find Jesus, living and expressed in the wonder of his creation, I may just fall in love with him in whole new ways. Recently I heard someone say that the miracle of Moses and the burning bush was not that the bush was burning; it was that Moses *saw* it, because Christ is burning in bushes everywhere. To read the Gospels with a creation-awareness is to see how much Jesus loved the world around him—the innocence and dependence of the lambs; the flowers of the field, the birds of the air; the wheat in the fields and the plants in the garden. All of these reflected his Father's beauty and care. As I find Christ all around me, I can and will fall more in love with him. And, as is always the case in true love, my heart will increasingly love what *he* loves.

---

35 John Scotus Eriugena (trans. Christopher Bamford), *The Voice of the Eagle*, (Lindisfarne Books, 2000) p.87

"For the beauty of the earth,
 For the glory of the skies,
 For the love which from our birth
 Over and around us lies."

(Folliott Sandford Pierpoint, 1864)

CHAPTER 3

Christ in the Old Testament

If Christ lives beyond the limits of time, space and matter, then surely he is present beyond the bounds of the New Testament. This may seem obvious, but over the past several centuries, much of the church has presented the Christ-story as beginning with angelic appearances in the first two chapters of Luke's Gospel. Perhaps this is an extension of the persistent impact of the rationalism of the Enlightenment that we briefly considered in the Introduction. It continues to be the dominant worldview of our day, a perspective that has confidence only in what can be verified through the five senses. In biblical teaching, this led to the ascension of the historical-critical method which downplays any interpretation of Scripture that goes beyond what the author's original intent was, and how the listeners would have understood that in light of their contemporary environment. Within this framework, there is very little room for mystery. Instead, it tells us that Jesus' story begins when he came to earth. Jesus, the Son of God, is somehow less than the Father. He is sent on assignment to fix a mess; the gospel is the story of how he went about doing that. This ignores the clear testimony of the Old Testament prophets, the apostles, and the early church. There never was a time without the Son. There never was a time when the Son was not at work, fulfilling the desires of the Father. This, of course, includes his activity throughout the Old Testament.

For too many years I read the OT with very little awareness of Christ. I saw the Old and New Testaments as two very distinct books—both are the inspired, infallible word of God, but fundamentally separated by the absence or presence of Christ. I read supernatural OT encounters as being with the Father or angels. Frankly, it didn't even occur to me to see Christ in these encounters. When I finally saw Christ in the OT, I saw him everywhere. The OT came to life as never before. It was suddenly a book beyond the confines of ancient history, expressing and reflecting his beauty. Martin Luther said it well: "Scripture is the cradle in which Christ lies."[36]

Prior to the 16th century Reformation, the church universally understood that Christ was present throughout all of the Old Testament. It was Christ who held the Scriptures together; apart from him there could be no real scriptural understanding. The apostles, following the example of Jesus on the Emmaus Road, taught the gospel by revealing Christ in the Old Testament. Ignatius, an early church father, declared his conviction that the Old Testament *is* Jesus Christ. "All Scripture pertaining to the revelation of God is identical with the revelation of God given in Christ as preached by the apostles, and

---

36 Leonard Sweet and Frank Viola, *Jesus: A Theography*, (Thomas Nelson, 2012) p.xv

in reverse, all that the Gospel proclaims has already been written down as Scripture."[37]

Jesus told the disciples that he is the door of the sheep, the door to the Father. Throughout the OT, we see Christ being the door of the patriarchs, Moses, Joshua, and the many others who encountered him, knowingly or unknowingly. Irenaeus wrote, "Anyone who reads the Scriptures attentively will find in them an account of Christ and a foreshadowing of the new calling, for Christ is the treasure hidden in the field."[38] Beyond being revealed at various times in the OT, the church fathers taught that everything written is about Christ. The OT is fulfilled in Christ; its promises and prophecies come to pass in his Incarnation. The OT points to Christ with a fundamental focus that is unwavering in its future perspective. While the OT looks forward to Christ, he is also eternally present in all of the Scriptures. They are not just *about* him; Christ is *in* them. Paul told the Galatians that the OT is a teacher that leads us to Christ (Gal 3:24). The true significance of the OT Scriptures can only be found when we read, examine and meditate upon them in the light of Christ. The entire Scriptures are His Story.

---

37   John Behr, St. Irenaeus, *On the Apostolic Preaching*, (Crestwood NY: St. Vladimir's Seminary Press, 1997) p.11

38   James R. Payton Jr., *Irenaeus on the Christian Faith*, (Eugene, Ore: Pickwick Publications, 2011) p.123

Who Was That?

During his exchange with Moses on Mount Sinai, God made an unequivocal statement: "You cannot see My face, for no one shall see me and live." (Ex 33:20) However, the Old Testament is filled with encounters where God *was* seen. Jacob wrestled with God; Moses spoke face to face with God; Samson's parents feared they would die because they had seen God. How can this be? It is John's revelation of the true identity of Jesus that gives us the answer: "In the beginning was the Word, and the Word was with God, and the Word was God." (Jn 1:1) John is clearly paralleling the first words of Genesis, "In the beginning," linking the OT with the gospel. Christ is inseparable from the beginning of creation and time. He is inseparable from the OT, and all its manifestations of God are the Word, the Son. As the writer to the Hebrews said, Jesus is the exact expression of God. When the Father wants to speak, he does so through his Son, who John identifies as the Word. (Think about this the next time you read, "the word of the Lord came to them.") To see Christ is to see the Triune God.

When we learn to see Christ present in all of Scripture from beginning to end, we will gain a greater understanding of the purposes of God built into the foundation of the cosmos. Paul called this the "summing up of all things in Christ." Jesus has always lived as the eternal Son, the Word, and second Person of the Trinity. In my journey, I have come to "see" Jesus, as the early believers did, walking through *all* the pages of my Bible. The Father was speaking through his Son when he had the famous exchange with Adam and Eve in the Garden (Gen 3). The

One who tells us to always abide, to remain in him (Jn 15), is the same One who cried out in pain for what was about to take place, "Where are you?" Abandonment in the Garden and abandonment by his closest friends at his trial—both suffered by Christ.

Christophanies

The early church understood that Christ quite literally appeared at various times throughout the OT. These manifestations of God the Son are called Christophanies. They prefigure the Incarnation, when he took on human flesh. The church father, John of Damascus said, "No one saw the divine nature, but rather the image and figure of what was yet to come. For the invisible Son and Word of God was to become truly Son."[39]

Various passages in the New Testament declare that the creation of all things happened through and by Christ the Son.

> *All things came into being through him, and without him not one thing came into being. (Jn 1:3)*

> *For in him all things in heaven and on earth were created, things visible and invisible, whether thrones or dominions or rulers or powers—all things have been created through him and for him. (Col 1:16)*

---

39   T. Bobosh citing John of Damascus, *Fraternized,* (https://frted. wordpress.com/2017/01/06)

But in these last days he has spoken to us by a Son, whom
he appointed heir of all things, through whom he also
created the worlds. (Heb 1:2)

Since John's Gospel tells us clearly that Christ is the
Word, he is the One who speaks forth creation. When God
said, "Let there be light," this was the first instance of
God speaking; it was God the Son—Christ—who spoke.

Christ appeared to Abraham several times in different
manifestations: as a Man (Gen 18) whom Abraham instinc-
tively knew was the Lord; as the "Voice of the Lord" (Gen
15 LXX); and as the Angel of the Lord. Christ appeared
as the Angel of the Lord twice to Hagar, to the Midianite
Balaam (Nu 22), to Gideon (Judges 6), to Samson's parents
(Judges 13), and to David and Zechariah.

The Angel of the Lord is by far the most common
manifestation of Christ. The early church Fathers referred
to Christ as an angel, which likely came from the LXX
translation[40] of Isaiah 9:6:

"For a Child is born to us, and a Son is given to us, whose
government is upon His shoulder: and His name is called
the Angel of Great Counsel."

---

40   *The LXX, or Septuagint, is a Greek translation of the OT compiled from*
earlier Hebrew texts around 400 BC. It was the translation used and
quoted by Jesus and the Apostles and was what the early church used for
hundreds of years. The Masoretic text was a Hebrew translation compiled
between about 700-1000 AD. It is the basis for most translations of the
Old Testament. Because of the bias of the Jewish rabbis (all translations
have bias), it has been noted that Christ's presence is often obscured or
diminished. The LXX is the translation of Jesus, Paul, and the early
church.

For many Biblical scholars, this passage refers to Christ, therefore it follows that he is the Angel of the Lord. Once this is seen, we begin to recognize Christ's appearing throughout the OT, which speaks of the Angel of the Lord at least 54 times.

When Abraham took Isaac up Mount Moriah to sacrifice him in obedience to God, it was the Angel of the Lord that called out to him, "Stop!" It was the compassionate Christ who appeared as the Angel of the Lord to a desperate Hagar in the wilderness. Likewise, it was Christ as the Angel of the Lord who told Moses, "I AM." In various Old Testament passages the Angel of the Lord is addressed and sometimes recognized as God. Significantly, after the Incarnation, the Angel of the Lord is never mentioned again.

Jacob's encounter with the Angel of the Lord (Gen 32) is important on several levels. He appears to Jacob as a man with whom he wrestles through the night. Jacob comes away from this with a new name, one the nation that came from him still bears: Israel. Secondly, Jacob is marked physically for the rest of his life by this encounter with the Angel. Finally, we see a foreshadowing of the Incarnation. Christ appears as a man, limited in size and strength; he engages in human activity *as a human*, never acting outside of that self-imposed limitation.

Jesus told the Pharisees, "If you believed Moses, you would believe me, for he wrote of me." (Jn 5:18) Clearly, Moses never wrote about Jesus by name, so what did he mean? This takes us back to the issue of interpretation. Contrary to the modern historical-critical view which says that we must limit ourselves to the author's original intent and what the original audience heard, for more than 1500 years, it was acknowledged that the Holy Spirit revealed deeper truths than even the original author realized. The New Testament writers clearly recognized Christ throughout Moses' writing. That is why Hebrews 11:26 states that it was Christ who was at work in Moses' life:

> *He considered abuse suffered for the Christ to be greater wealth than the treasures of Egypt, for he was looking ahead to the reward.*

And Jude 5 tells us that it was Jesus who saved the Israelites from their bondage in Egypt. Paul recognized that Christ was with the Israelites in the desert:

> *[T]hey all drank the same spiritual drink. For they drank from a spiritual rock that followed them, and that rock was Christ. (1 Cor 10:4 CSB)*

This leads us to another way in which Christ is present throughout the OT.

Types

We can define a *type* as a "prophetic symbol" because all types found in the Bible are archetypes, or representations of something yet future. More specifically, a type in Scripture is a person, event, place, or thing in the Old Testament that foreshadows a person or thing in the New Testament. For example, the flood of Noah's day is used as a type of baptism.[41]

---

41   https://www.gotquestions.org/typology-Biblical.html

In studying types we must not fall into either of two errors: seeing types everywhere, which leads to a purely allegorical view of Scripture; conversely, we must not fall off on the other side, as the evangelical church has often done.

> "Because we tend to regard the time period of the biblical author and our own small moment under the sun as two distinct or separate moments, univocally (that is, having only one meaning) identical in kind, we believe that it is our job simply to find out what exactly the biblical author meant in any given biblical text in order then to proclaim it as authoritative."[42]

By elevating the historical-critical method many have resisted seeing a deeper meaning in Scripture passages, thus limiting everything to a purely rational and natural level.

Types reveal a greater truth, shifting our understanding from the material to the spiritual, from the earthly to the heavenly. As Jesus said to Nicodemus, "If I have told you earthly things and you do not believe, how will you believe if I tell you heavenly things?" (Jn 3:12 ESV)

Once we see Christ in types, his presence comes alive to us in the OT. This is a huge topic, too big for our scope here; however a few examples may help us in our journey of discovering Christ in all of Scripture.

---

42 Hans Boersma, *Heavenly Participation,* (Wm B. Eerdmans Pub, 2011) p.129

People as Types of Christ

Adam may be the most obvious example of a type in the Bible; Paul refers to Christ as the second Adam. Just as Adam introduced sin and death into the world, Christ brought forgiveness, reconciliation and eternal life. In Genesis 14 Abraham encounters Melchizedek, a mysterious character about whom all we know is that he is the King of Salem and a priest. On the surface, this brief episode may seem almost trivial. In the messianic, and most often quoted Psalm in the New Testament, David declares: "You are a priest forever according to the order of Melchizedek." (Ps 110:4) The writer to the Hebrews highlights at length that Melchizedek is a type of Christ. Some believers hold that Melchizedek is actually a Christophany. How was this type fulfilled? Like Jesus, he was:

Having neither beginning of days nor end of life, but resembling the Son of God, he remains a priest forever. (Heb 7:3)

Moses, in his unique role of prophet, leader, and mediator for the people of God, was a type of Jesus; the One who functions forever in a similar, though infinitely more exalted capacity. In Jesus' day, this Mosaic connection was recognized by John the Baptist when his followers asked, "Are you the Coming One?" referring specifically to the messianic promise that God would send Israel someone who would be like Moses (Dt 18:15). Likewise after Jesus' resurrection, both Peter and Stephen specifically pointed to this promise when they called the people to repent and turn their hearts and lives to Christ. There are many other Old Testament people who are types of Christ, including Joseph, Joshua and David. When we begin to recognize them as such, their actions and words take on greater significance, pointing beyond themselves to where they find their ultimate meaning as pre-incarnations of Christ.

Objects as Types

Jesus manifests his presence through physical objects. When we begin to see this, we read the Scriptures with a new vividness, helping us to enter the story ourselves, experiencing the "eternal now" of what is taking place. In Genesis 28, Jacob has just hurriedly left home for Mesopotamia. Through his own deceitfulness, Jacob has kindled in his brother a murderous rage; likely his father's affection had turned away from Jacob. Imagine his emotions on that first night of his long journey. Fear, confusion, regret, uncertainty, abandonment washed over him as he tried to sleep. It was into this state that Christ intervened. As he slept, Jacob saw a vision of a ladder between earth and heaven with angels ascending and descending. To this day, many theologians of the patristic tradition (the study of the early church fathers) teach that the ladder is Christ himself. At his lowest moment, Jacob encounters the compassionate One. About 1500 years later, this same Jesus refers Nathaniel to the same ladder with the same promise of angelic, heavenly activity (Jn 1:51). Christ beyond time. We are invited to move beyond reading about past events to participating in them.

There are many more examples of objects that point to Christ, for example, the bronze snake in the desert that foreshadowed Jesus' being lifted up on a cross; the "watering" rock in the desert; the ark and the Holy of Holies. Recognizing Christ in these types expands the OT, in some ways moving it from Israel's past to our present.

Places as Types

Three places stand out above all others as geographical types with great allegorical significance. Egypt represents our old life. It is a place of bondage that holds us captive prior to turning to Christ. Second, Jerusalem (Zion) typifies the church, Christ's bride, and our final destination: a new heaven and earth. Conversely, Babylon, which held God's people captive for 70 years, is a picture of aggression, violence, and evil. This is especially prevalent in Revelation (11:8; 14:8; 16:19; 17:5; 18:2). During seasons of church persecution, Babylon was code for Rome.

Events as Types

Listing a number of key events in Israel's history, Paul told the Corinthians, "These things happened to them to serve as an example, and they were written down to instruct us, on whom the ends of the ages have come." (1 Cor 10:11) Beyond serving as a warning, these events are points of contemplation that can draw believers into greater awareness of God's eternal purposes for the cosmos through the second Person of the Trinity. We can read the story of the parting of the Red Sea and think, "Wasn't that amazing!" Alternatively, we can see Christ in the center of this event, delivering them from Egypt with his great joy, anticipating the rescue of the whole world from death to life. Jesus gave them manna to eat, and so it is no wonder he announced to the Jews 1300 years later that he is the Bread of Life. With an awareness of Christ, I cannot help but read this miracle in a new, bigger way, where past and present merge. Christ was with Noah and his family in the ark ("in him *all things* hold together" Col 1:17) and at the same time he was expressing the deliverance that would be for all mankind, represented through baptism. Past, present and future all held together by Christ.

Types: Looking Deeper

It is important to be aware that types were not only symbols anticipating the Incarnation of Christ; in and of themselves, they were ever-present activities of the Triune God who is always at work in salvation history.

> "The manna, for example, was not just a picture or symbol of a future reality that would some day come into existence, that is, Christ as the bread of life … Christ was already sacramentally present in the manna."[43]

For many of us, OT teaching about Christ was singularly focused upon how he fulfilled prophecy. The value of various passages was found in how they pointed *forward*. However, Christ is not just the destination toward which the OT points; he indwells the OT in a way that transcends time. That is why Jesus not only told the

---

43   Craig Carter, *Interpreting Scripture With the Great Tradition,* (Baker Academic, 2018) p.175

Pharisees that "before Abraham was, I AM," but also said, "Your ancestor Abraham rejoiced that he would see my day; he saw it and was glad." (Jn 8:56)

When we begin to see the OT through the lens of sacramental time where Christ actively and tangibly exists in past, present and future, we begin to experience Christ first-hand, with a growing awareness of his living presence in the now of what we formerly thought as simply happening in the past.

> "Christ is never absent from salvation history; he
> is with his people, saving and sanctifying them at
> every point of time simultaneously."[44]

We have already noted that it was Christ, the Angel of the Lord, who called out to Abraham on Mount Moriah to not kill his son Isaac. We can also easily see that his sacrifice was a type of Christ's sacrifice. Isaac was the child of promise, through whom God would create a people for himself. But now let's go deeper. Sacramental time is not sequential in its essence (although it may initially be experienced that way). Isaac's sacrifice does not just look ahead to Christ's crucifixion; it is directly connected to it. Both events are linked in God's great plan to have a people—a bride—for himself. Because of Christ's presence in the midst of this event in time and space, Isaac's sacrifice is more than a type—it is participation in the crucifixion.

> "Christ himself, we could say, is *the* great sacrament,
> the mystery par excellence. In him, the eternal Word

---

44   ibid

enters into the temporal succession of events, thus allowing time to participate sacramentally in eternity ... Temporal events have meaning because of their sacramental connection ... to the incarnate Logos, Jesus Christ himself."[45]

As noted earlier, St. Ignatius, one of the very early church Fathers, stated that the Old Testament *is* Jesus Christ. He did not mean that Christ was a higher revelation or a replacement for the OT; rather, he meant that the OT was the Word made flesh. Not only did the OT point to Christ; not only did Christ appear at various times in the OT; it is Christ who indwells the OT, giving it eternal, ultimate meaning. Conversely, there is a reciprocity in Christ's relationship with the OT, for as the Old Testament looks forward, it gives layers of meaning to the Gospels and the entire New Testament. St. Irenaeus gives a wonderful example of this:

> "The rejoicing of Abraham descended upon those who sprang from him ... while on the other hand, there was a reciprocal rejoicing which passed backwards from the children to Abraham who did also desire to see the day of Christ's coming. Rightly then, did our Lord bear witness to him, saying 'Your father Abraham rejoiced to see my day; he saw it and was glad.' (Jn 8:56)"[46]

---

45   Hans Boersma, *Heavenly Participation*, p.127
46   John Behr, St. Irenaeus, *On the Apostolic Preaching*, (St. Vladimir's Seminary Press, 1997)

The study of various Old Testament types can be a helpful Bible study tool; however, it comes with an inherent danger. We can see types as a way of understanding more about Jesus, which is helpful, but limiting. More than markers, indicating where Christ shows up in the OT story, types (as is true for all of the OT) invite us to deeply connect with Jesus, moving us from knowing more *about* him, to *knowing* him. This is an important shift; we can easily be led by our curiosity to understand Jesus better. We can be satisfied to recognize him through various types. However, he invites us to enter the Old Testament *with* him, to participate with him in its pages. How are we granted this remarkable invitation? It is because Jesus and especially Paul have clearly said that we are "in him." Where he goes, we are always invited to follow. This has forever changed the way I read the OT. As I read its pages, I can *feel* him, his presence tangible and strong; I find myself interacting with him in silent conversation as I "see" Abraham, Moses, David, and others. The OT is not ancient history: it is living history right now. Jesus invites me into his eternal "now."

As I increasingly experience Christ in the pillar of cloud and fire, I feel new depths of knowing him as the protector and guide in history who today protects and guides *me*. Christ the all-powerful One who comes down onto Mount Sinai, who causes the Israelites to fall on their faces in the presence of such power, is the same Jesus who comes "gentle and lowly." Without knowing him in awesome power, how could I ever realize the wonder of his coming in such humility and obedience? How could I ever understand that Christ, who emptied himself on the Cross, is the highest revelation of who he really is?

Since the beginning of the church, the Psalms have been its prayerbook and hymnbook. Many of us have included the Psalms in our daily reading. The great tradition of the church fathers and mothers insisted that each Psalm in some way discloses Christ. Reading them through the lens of Christ has opened up new levels of meaning that I had never seen before. Psalm One begins, "Blessed is the man ... he shall be like a tree planted by streams of waters that produces its fruit in its season" (Ps 1:1,3 LXX); this man is Christ who is like a tree that protects and brings life to us. In Psalm Two Christ declares that he was established as King by the Father. In Psalm Three we hear the very real human pain that Jesus felt when he was attacked, and how he "lay down and slept; I awoke for the Lord will help me." And so on, and so on, throughout 150 Psalms. These give me fresh fuel for contemplating Christ.

As Bradley Jersak points out in *A More Christlike Word*, the superscriptions at the top of many psalms read, "for the choir director." This is a translation from the Masoretic text which we have learned was compiled more than 700 years after Christ. Christ, the Apostles, and the early church would have instead read and taught from the Septuagint (LXX). This was their Bible (which is why I use it for my daily reading). In this translation, "for the choir director" becomes, "to the end." What does that mean? Christ is the end of all things, the *telos*, the summing up of God's great purpose for all of creation for all time. *Christ* is the end of all things, who opens up the Psalms.

Christ is the interpretive key that opens up the OT. We start to read, not looking back to the past from a distance, but encountering Jesus in real time. More than recognizing types or prophecies (as valuable as these are), we are experiencing him in the moment. Jesus is encountering Adam and Eve—and me—in the Garden, speaking right now. Jesus is meeting both Elijah and me in the midst of our fear and discouragement. When Jesus speaks to Elijah outside the cave, this is more than an example for me to learn from. Jesus is eternally in the midst of that exchange; therefore, he is strengthening me right now just as he is strengthening Elijah through a present encounter.

When preaching the Gospel overseas, I have pointed people to John 10:10; "The thief comes to steal, kill and destroy, but I have come that you might have abundant life." I want people, especially those with no Christian context, to understand that it is their enemy, the Satan, who opposes them; it is not God who is somehow punishing them. For many years I have struggled with the violence, even genocide in the OT, especially that committed by the Israelites. How can this point me to Christ? Where can I find him in this? He is love. Full stop. He is never violent toward anyone. However, he suffered terrible violence. So when I read about violence, injustice and suffering in the OT, they direct me to Jesus on the cross, stirring a deeper awareness of what he suffered on our behalf. I remember that it was not the anger or violence of the Father that put Jesus on the cross; it was the anger and violence of people.

It is because of the life of Christ in us that we can ask the Holy Spirit, whenever we open the Scriptures, to reveal Jesus to us. This is not from the distance of ordinary, chronological time, but from the vivid reality of sacramental time in which we encounter Jesus in the eternal now of the Old Testament.

Long ago, St. Augustine wrote:

"At that time the New Testament was hidden within the Old, as fruit is in the root ... Christ himself, inasmuch as he was to be born according to the flesh, was hidden in the root, that is to say, in the bloodline of the patriarchs. At the appointed time he was to be revealed, like fruit forming from the flower, and so Scripture says, '*A shoot has sprung from Jesse's stock, and a flower has opened.*'"[47]

The OT looks prophetically forward to Christ. The NT writers look backward for OT fulfillment. Christ is in both. But he also continues, across and beyond time, in the vitality of a present that will have no end. A bigger Christ. A bigger gospel.

* * *

Then he opened their minds to understand the scriptures. (Lu 24:45)

Christ, the timeless One, lives in the Old Testament. Yes, he can be found in Christophanies, prefigured in events,

---

47   Augustine, *Expositions of the Psalms*, cited by Craig Carter, *Interpreting Scripture with the Great Tradition*, p.159

people and objects, in the Psalms, and many other places. But more than searching for evidence of him in all of these, he, the Word that spoke and is still speaking, is the lens through which we are to read the Scriptures. Even more than a lens, Christ is the very breath of the Old and New Testaments. Rather than looking for clues of his whereabouts like a detective, Jesus invites us to enter into the Scriptures (which he declared as holy and inviolable in Matthew 5:18) *with* him, experiencing him there. Not finding out more about him, but entering into his eternal activity, often in surprising ways and places. Not merely the object of my search, but a guide on the journey, he says to me, "Did you see that? What do you think about that? Look over here!" He illuminates each passage. Sometimes this is by way of contrast with what I am reading. If Christ is the full revelation of the Triune God and God is always love (1 Jn 4:8), then when we read about slaughter against other nations, these narratives stand in stark contrast, and point us back to Christ's true nature.

Jesus confronted the scribes and the Pharisees, people who had dedicated themselves to studying the depths of the Scriptures.

> *You search the Scriptures because you think they give you eternal life. But the Scriptures point to me!*
> *(Jn 5:39, NLT)*

Surely they were sincere and diligent, but it seems that they were missing the most important thing: Jesus' presence in the Scriptures. The Old Testament does not just point to Jesus; more than this, it *reveals* him—and conversely, Jesus reveals the Old Testament. It is His

Spirit alive in us that connects us to the Scriptures at a deeper level. The church father Origen wrote that if we only understand a verse or passage at its literal level, then we do not yet truly understand it. He insisted that each verse carries a mystical, water-to-wine meaning that reveals truth about Christ. It is his actual and timeless presence that gives eternal significance to an event that goes beyond the actual event itself.

The Old Testament invites me into a progressive understanding. There comes a day when I see Christ in its pages; soon I see him everywhere. He has become the interpretive key, the lens through which I read the Old Testament. From here I begin to see and sense his presence as I read; beyond this, there are times when I know Jesus next to me, not only guiding me as I read and consider, but reading *with* me. Perhaps this is something of what the two disciples experienced on the Emmaus Road. Over the years of this journey, my Bible has somehow gotten thicker, fuller, more wonderful, and more alive.

CHAPTER 4

Into The Heart of the Mystery

"The Son is the radiance of God's glory and the exact expression of His nature, sustaining all things by His powerful word." (Heb 1:3 CSB)

In seeking greater insight into the mystery of Christ, we now turn to what is at its heart; the Incarnation undergirds everything we will ever understand about Christ. Its implications are so wide-reaching that it is difficult to even know the limits of its examination because the Incarnation impacts everything: the relationship between God and man; salvation; suffering; the Cross; the creation; and reconciliation of the universe. The Incarnation stands at the center of the New Testament message, that the Divine Son of God has come in the flesh.

> "Everything in Christianity centers on the incarnation of the Son of God, an invasion of God among men and women in time, bringing and working out a salvation not only understandable by them in their own historical and human life and existence, but historically and concretely accessible to them on earth and in time"[48]

---

48   T.F. Torrance, *Incarnation*, (IVP Academic, 2015) p.8

The doctrine of the Incarnation expresses the mystery that Jesus Christ is fully human and fully God. This union of God and man is not merely a spiritual union; it is a physical union of two natures so as to make one Person. Jesus Christ did not set aside his divinity in order to come "dwell among us." The Apostle John, recognizing the centrality of the Incarnation, began his Gospel with a poetic description:

In the beginning was the Word, and the Word was with God, and the Word was God ... And the Word became flesh and lived among us. (Jn 1:1,14)

St. Augustine called these "the most sublime words ever penned." With just a few words, John brings to us the truth of Jesus Christ as fully God and at the same time, fully man. John insists upon this truth which is at the heart of all that he wrote in both his Gospel and first letter.

We declare to you what was from the beginning, what we have heard, what we have seen with our eyes, what we have looked at and touched with our hands, concerning the Word of life — this life was revealed, and we have seen it and testify to it and declare to you the eternal life that was with the Father and was revealed to us. (1 Jn 1:1-2)

From the earliest days of the church, the Incarnation has been a non-negotiable, foundational tenet of the faith. It was taught, preached and wrestled over; in short, the Incarnation was central to the Christian faith. And yet, all too often in our day, it has come to mean little more than what we sing about on Christmas Eve without meditating upon its ultimate significance.

"The Incarnation [is] identified as the moment when
the love of God for human beings reveals itself to the
highest degree and when human beings are called,
in turn, to respond to the love of God with their own
love for God."[49]

God's infinite love is the heartbeat of the Incarnation.
It answers the great "why." Underlying everything is the
unfathomable, relentless love of God. He never has given
up on us, nor will he ever. The Incarnation is a reflection
of that love.

God's Purpose and Plan

Perhaps no church father wrote more about the Incarnation
than St. Athanasius. At a time when orthodoxy was being
threatened from many directions, Athanasius clearly
articulated the centrality of Jesus Christ's humanity and
divinity. He wrote,

"He did two things: He put an end to the law of death
which barred our way; and he made a new beginning
of life for us, by giving us the hope of resurrection.
There were thus two things which the Savior did for
us by becoming Man. He banished death from us
and made us anew; and ... he became visible through
His works and revealed Himself as the Word of the
Father, the Ruler and King of the whole creation."[50]

---

49   Hilarion Alfeyev, *The Spiritual World of Isaac the Syrian*, (Cisterian
      Publications 2000) p.49

50   St. Athanasius, *On the Incarnation*, (Pantianos Classics, 2016)
      p.24,32-33

Many books have been written about God's purpose for the Incarnation. Broadly speaking, they fall into one of two categories: Christ came to earth to redeem mankind, or he came to reveal the love of the Father. Both of these perspectives lead directly to the question of whether the Incarnation was always the Triune God's plan, or did it only become necessary because of the Fall.

In the West, Thomas Aquinas was the leading theologian of the Middle Ages and to this day is considered the foremost teacher in the Catholic Church. He taught that "the work of the Incarnation was ordained as a remedy for sin, so that, if sin had not existed, the Incarnation would never have taken place."[51] Seven hundred years later, the majority of the Catholic Church has not moved away from this position. They teach that because of the original sin of Adam, humanity has fallen away and was doomed to separation from God. God's remedy for this was to come to mankind in the Incarnation. This view presupposes that the Incarnation was not God's original plan, which may lead us to imagine that it was not his best. Rather, it was God's response to repair that which was broken.

However, God is love. His infinite and eternal love is his full identity and motivation. Therefore, his love is infinitely greater than sin, including Adam's. To believe that sin would lead God to become incarnate in order to repair the damage caused by humankind would be to give sin the power to determine God's actions; however, God is always completely free in his love and actions.

---

51   https://www.newadvent.org/summa

Writing just forty years after Aquinas, John Duns Scotus had much to say about God's purpose for creation. He insisted that for all eternity the Triune God freely chose to create, and then to enter the universe. Why? Because of his great love. The universe was created so that God would have another way to be love and to express that love to another beloved. The Trinity conceived the universe with the plan that the human race would come into the privileged position of God's physical entry point into the universe.[52]

Hundreds of years before Aquinas, the fathers and mothers of the Church consistently taught that the Incarnation would have happened without the Fall. St. Isaac the Syrian wrote that God's purpose for the Incarnation was based upon his great love for humanity (Jn 3:16), not saving humanity from sin. For Isaac, the Incarnation happened

> "not to redeem us from sins, or for any other reason,
> but solely in order that the world might become
> aware of the love which God has for his creation."[53]

The Incarnation is the moment in time and space whereby God's love for humanity reveals itself to the highest possible degree. The Second Person, the Creator of the cosmos, enters into and becomes part of his creation, with all of its brokenness and pain. And why? To complete

---

52 Franciscan Media, *St. Francis and the Incarnation*, (https://www.franciscanmedia.org/franciscan-spirit-blog/st-francis-and-the-incarnation/)

53 St. Isaac, Gnostic Chapters IV, 78 cited by Hilarion Alfeyev, *The Spiritual World of Isaac the Syrian*, (Cistercian Publications, 2000) p.52

some sort of cosmic legal transaction, or to tell humanity what a mess it has made of everything? No, he came for only one reason: to reveal to us the relentless, unlimited, unconditional love he has for us. In the Incarnation, God took the initiative; his great purpose was to establish full, unbroken communion between himself and humanity. As Irenaeus wrote, "How could the human race go to God if God had not come to us?"

Deification

Another church father, Maximus, was convinced that the Incarnation would happen even without the Fall, but for a different reason, going back to God's original intention of the entire universe being consummated in Christ. This would mean making all of humanity divine through perfect union with Christ. This was often written about by the church fathers; among others, Irenaeus, Athanasius, and Gregory of Nyssa all said that God became man in order that man might become God. Irenaeus said that God had "become what we are, that he might bring us to be even what he is himself." Although we may struggle with this, even Jesus said to the Pharisees: "Is it not written in your law, 'I said, you are gods'?" (Jn 10:34)

This is called *deification* and it was a major focus of teaching for the first several hundred years of the church. In order to understand deification more fully, it is important that we consider the two dimensions of God's relationship with us: his essence and his energies. His *essence* refers to God's inner being and nature: his otherness. His *energies* are his acts of power, how he operates in the world. His energies refer to his immanence and omnipresence, God in his self-revelation.

"While God's inner essence is forever beyond our comprehension, His energies, grace, life and power fill the whole universe, and are directly accessible to us."[54]

What the church was *not* saying is that as Christians we eventually become like God in his essence (his uncreated being that subsists by itself). We will never be like him in his essence: that is why he is unapproachable. However, we can and do approach him in his energies.

In his Prologue, the Apostle John wrote, "From his fullness we have all received grace upon grace." (Jn 1:16) Similarly, Paul wrote to the Ephesians, "to know the love of Christ that surpasses knowledge, so that you may be filled with all the fullness of God." (3:19) This is how we become more like God: it is by his divine energies, his grace working in us. When Christ assumed our identity, the *process of reversal and renewal began.* This is why Paul wrote, "You are a new creation." (2 Cor 5:17) Because of the Incarnation, because the fullness of God inhabited human flesh, it was now possible for us to begin the journey into our final destiny; to become perfectly unified with God, becoming by grace (his empowering presence) what Christ is by nature. That is why Peter wrote: "you may become partakers of the divine nature." (2 Pe 1:4)

It is the energies of God that enable us to experience, right now, something of the Divine through sensory

---

54   Kallistos Ware, *The Orthodox Way*, (St, Vladimir's Seminary Press, 1979) p.22

perception and intuition. Christians are those who are incarnating Christ in their own bodies due to the indwelling and transforming Spirit of Christ that lives within them. When Paul said that we are being conformed into the image of Christ, he did not just mean that we were to imitate his life morally. Rather, his God-ness is powerfully at work in us, making us, in the core of our being, more and more like him. Deification insists that we are, in a deep and mysterious way, "in Christ."

> "If there is any reason why Christ was born, crucified, and resurrected, it is this: so that we may become what He is."[55]

God descends to the world and becomes man, and through this action of God's love, man is raised toward his true destiny: to be united with Christ. If the Fall had not taken place, Christ would have become incarnate in order to unite humanity with himself. For the Incarnation was not some sort of rescue plan, but the greatest expression of the purely giving love of God.

> "When God, who is absolute fullness, brought creatures into existence, it was not done to fulfill any need but so that his creatures should be happy to share his likeness and so that he himself might rejoice in the joy of his creatures as they draw inexhaustibly upon the Inexhaustible."[56]

55　Archimandrite Aimilianos, *The Way of the Spirit*, (Indicts Publishing, 2008) p.156

56　Olivier Clement, *The Roots of Christian Mysticism*, (New City Press, 1995), p.32

Elsewhere, Maximus expresses the Incarnation through an even more expansive cosmological lens:

> "Maximus sees the fall and reconciliation of man as a smaller arch in the larger story of God's plan. That plan which 'pre-existed the ages' is the movement of the Creator wishing to unite his creation with himself. He wishes to share his divine life, and the way that he does this is to be hypostatically united to man."[57]

This view reinforces Paul's insistence in Ephesians 1:10 that in Christ is the "summing up of all things." Contemplation of the Incarnation leads us to ever-broader horizons of its eternal significance, as Maximus wrote extensively in *On the Cosmic Mystery of Jesus Christ*.

Why Did Christ Come? Two Views

Ultimately, it makes a great difference whether we understand the Incarnation as God's response to the Fall of man, or that it was always part of his original plan. Our understanding becomes the lens through which we see all of God's acts, from creation to the Cross and beyond. Did the Fall happen outside of God's control? Did Christ come to invite us home or to show us how far we have fallen? Is the purpose of the Cross to punish sin or to heal it? A right and healthy relationship with the Triune God flows from a right understanding of the Incarnation.

---

57 Joseph Healy, *St. Maximus the Confessor on Why God Became Man*, (https://www.wordonfire.org/articles/st-maximus-the-confessor-on-why-god-became-man) Dec. 2023

Beyond this, there are other reasons for the Incarnation. Jesus came to reveal God to humanity. He is the full and perfect expression of the Triune God.

He is the reflection of God's glory and the exact imprint of God's very being (Heb 1:3)

This was a dividing revelation; for many, Jesus was the embodiment of good news. For others, he deeply threatened their existing view of God and so he was rejected. Secondly, Jesus came to reveal life as it was created to be in the mind of God. He came not only to model this kind of life, but to empower us to live it. In John 10:10, he called this gift *abundant life.* Thirdly, Jesus came to defeat the power of the evil one.

Since, therefore, the children share flesh and blood, he himself likewise shared the same things, so that through death he might destroy the one who has the power of death, that is, the devil, and free those who all their lives were held in slavery by the fear of death. (Heb 2:14-15)

Fourthly, through the Incarnation, Jesus came to redeem and rescue us. This was always God's plan from before the beginning of time. Through the Incarnation, that plan was put into action.

But when the fullness of time had come, God sent his Son, born of a woman, born under the law, in order to redeem those who were under the law, so that we might receive adoption as children. (Gal 4:4-5)

Union of God and Man

"God's own Son was made the Son of man so that
he might make the sons of men the sons of God."
(St. Chrysostom)

In considering the incarnation, it is of great importance that we understand that Jesus does everything as *One Person* in his united natures. He is not two beings operating in one body. His divine and human natures are always fully united, and therefore never operate separately because this would divide the God-Man union. From the earliest days, what has challenged theologians is to understand how there is only one person acting at all times. To help clarify this they asked, "Did Jesus walk on water?" Yes. "Did he do it in his divine nature?" Yes. People can't walk on water. Then they posed the problem, "Walked? God doesn't have feet." He simply walked on water. And this suggests he is divine and human. Likewise, God died in the flesh; If he's not human, he can't die. If he's not God, he just dies. But Jesus, in the fullness of his one being, in both his indivisible natures, conquers death. The issue is not just that he dies as a human and conquers death as divine. This can only happen if he's always both.[58] This understanding is the grid through which we can pursue the mystery of the Incarnation.

The best known verse in the Scriptures about the Incarnation is almost certainly John 1:14.

---

58   Personal correspondence with Dr. Bradley Jersak, January 2024

And the Word became flesh and lived among us, and we have seen his glory, the glory as of a father's only son, full of grace and truth.

"The Word became flesh." The meaning of the Apostle John's words have fueled multiple church councils, books, articles and debates spanning centuries that continue to this day. At the center of the church council debates was the nature of the union of God and man in Jesus Christ. This union was difficult to understand at a deep level without breaking the dynamic tension held within it. Primarily, one group denied the full deity of Christ as the eternal Son of God who is one with the Father (*Arianism*), while another group denied his humanity, teaching that Christ only appeared to be human (*Docetism*).

As Dr. Cherith Nordling has said,

> If we give even the slightest bit on either side of those, the story falls apart. We don't have God present to us, and I can't really trust that my humanity is redeemed and whole and kept in the presence of God by somebody who knows my story intimately and is *for me* in that story.[59]

The rise of Arianism created a huge crisis in the church, threatening to tear it into two. In response, leaders gathered in 325 A.D. and again in 381 to wrestle with the issue of the humanity and divinity of Christ. The great historic result was the Nicene Creed, which to this

---

59   Cherith Nordling, (https://learn.gcs.edu/mod/page/view. php?id=4423)

day is said weekly in the majority of churches around the world, declaring the unity of Christ.

> We believe in one Lord, Jesus Christ, the only Son of God, eternally begotten of the Father, God from God, Light from Light, true God from true God, begotten, not made, of one Being with the Father …
> By the power of the Holy Spirit
> He became incarnate from the Virgin Mary, and was made man.

Hypostasis

The union of Christ, in one person, fully human and fully divine, is known as *hypostasis*. The second Person of the Trinity, "God from God" came in human flesh. Jesus Christ's humanity is as full and real as it is in all of us. And just as fully, he is God, the creator of the universe who holds everything together. While he was healing the leper, raising Lazarus to life, feeding the five thousand, at the same moment, in his united humanity and divinity, Jesus was orchestrating, creating and continuing to create the entire universe. As Kenneth Tanner has said, "The One who is held in Mary's arms simultaneously holds the cosmos in his hands." How can we ever understand this? No wonder the church struggled to find words to adequately express this mystery. Often it used language expressing two natures of Christ—human and divine. The union of God and Man is not merely a moral or spiritual union; it is a *complete* union of two natures in One Eternal

Person.[60] We must be careful not to pass over this great mystery too quickly, thinking that we understand it. But as we, again and again, take time to contemplate this union, all we can do is recognize a wonder that is truly beyond us. Fifteen hundred years ago, St. Isaac wrote:

> "O wonder! The Creator clothed in human being enters the house of tax collectors and prostitutes, and when they turn toward him—through his own action—he was urging them, providing them by means of his teaching with assurance and reconciliation with him … Thus the entire universe through the beauty of the sight of him, was drawn by his love to the single confession of God, the Lord of all, and so the knowledge of the one Creator was sown everywhere."[61]

We are dealing with a mystery that is beyond our ability to fully comprehend and therefore, all of our language is inadequate. Some mysteries need to be embraced more than explained.

Heaven and Earth Connected

The Incarnation brought a new reality into being. Because Jesus Christ is both fully God and Man, when he entered the world in Bethlehem, for the first time heaven and earth were connected. Throughout the Old Testament

---

60   Christ is fully God and man in one person, not a 50-50 hybrid of God and man.

61   St. Isaac, Gnostic Chapters IV, 78 cited by Hilarion Alfeyev, *The Spiritual World of Isaac the Syrian*, (Cistercian Publications, 2000) p.55-6

there were isolated moments when the power and presence of heaven broke into the earthly realm, but now both realities were permanently joined.

There is a marvelous episode in John's Gospel. Jesus calls out to Nathaniel, a friend of Philip's that he has never met. When Nathaniel claims a case of mistaken identity, Jesus tells him that before Nathaniel had ever come near, Jesus "saw" him in another location. Nathaniel's response to this is powerful: "You are the Son of God!" Jesus then speaks words full of incarnational meaning: "Very truly, I tell you, you will see heaven opened and the angels of God ascending and descending upon the Son of Man." (Jn 1:51) Jesus is referring to an episode in Genesis 28 when Jacob saw a ladder connecting heaven and earth, with angels ascending and descending upon it. What was a one-time event for Jacob would, because of the union of God and man in one person, become the new, universal reality. Urs von Balthasar points out the significance of Jesus' words to Nathaniel. Heaven is now open to the world. Jesus has, through the Incarnation, made the exchange between heaven and earth possible.[62]

> "The temporary stairway between earth and heaven that Jacob witnessed in Old Testament times has given way to the permanence of the Word enfleshed as the link between the human and the divine. There is a bridge between heaven and earth that was not there before. In Pauline language the mediator has come."[63]

---

62 Graham Cole, *The God Who Became Human*, (InterVarsity Press, 2013) p.123

63 ibid

There is one God; there is also one mediator between God and humankind, Christ Jesus, himself human (1 Tim 2:5). Jesus brought the substance of heaven to the earth. Through the Incarnation, the infinite and finite resided in one Person. When Christ entered human existence, the unlimited and limited came together. Creation's relation to God ... is grounded in the Son's relation to the Father.[64] This is why Paul describes Christ's obedience to the Father as emptying Himself. He *chose* to limit Himself.

In his humanity, Jesus showed us how to live according to God's intention for us. He told the disciples to follow him, in large part to be a model for this true and abundant life. But beyond providing a model, Jesus brought a new power into their, and our, lives. Through the Holy Spirit, he implanted and released this true life that finds its source in the reality of heaven. This true life is found in him; everything else is incomplete.

For this reason the Apostle John continually calls us into this incarnate, human-God life. In John 15, Jesus tells the disciples to abide in him. This is so central that John uses the Greek word for abide, *meno*, 63 times throughout his Gospel and 18 more times in his short letter. Before the Incarnation, this kind of intimacy with God was beyond the reach of people. But after the birth, death, resurrection and ascension we are invited into Christ's incarnational life. This truth was so central to Paul that he wrote about being "in Christ" 164 times, for this is our truest identity. Both John and Paul are inviting and exhorting the churches and us to live daily in the reality of the Incarnation.

____

64   Rowan Williams, *Christ the Heart of Creation*, (Bloomsbury Continuum, 2018) p.221

The Humanity of Christ[65]

All that Jesus did in the historical setting of first century Palestine, as a citizen of an occupied and poor nation, he did as a man. To say that the reason he healed the sick and performed miracles was because he was divine, rather than as an expression of his perfect, undefiled humanity, is to break the connection of his God-man existence.

> "Here in Jesus the eternal God comes so near that he is a particular man among others, a particular historical individual, a frail human being, such a man in fact that people could easily pass him by as just another man, and easily fail to see anything else in him than ordinary humanity."[66]

When the Word became flesh, God was immersed in humanity and the natural world. "Jesus breathes the same air as all the living creatures on Earth, eats food grown from the same ground and drinks water from the same raindrops. The natural biological processes of human flesh are true of the man Jesus. Jesus smells, tastes and feels in the same way that all humans do. In Jesus, God joins the web of life and becomes part of Earth's biology."[67]

As humans, we exist in nature and are part of nature. We live in the midst, and as members, of an interdependent creation. Through the Incarnation, God the Son immersed himself in this Creation, became a part of it, and therefore displayed the Triune God *through* creation.

---

65   I am indebted to Dr. Cherith Nordling for her insights presented on the Impact Nations podcast, April 6, 2023

66   T.F. Torrance, *Incarnation*, (IVP Academic, 2008) p.185

67   Cherith Nordling, ibid

Speaking generally, when Jesus is called the Son of God, it is a reflection of his Deity as the second Person in the Trinity; and the Son of Man, in his humanity. It is interesting that Jesus referred to himself almost exclusively as the Son of Man, in fact, over 80 times in the Gospels. There were a number of references to "son of man" in the Old Testament, most significantly in Daniel 7.

I was watching in the night visions,
And behold, One like the Son of Man,
Coming with the clouds of heaven!
He came to the Ancient of Days,
And they brought Him near before Him.
Then to Him was given dominion and glory and a
kingdom,
That all peoples, nations, and languages should serve Him.
His dominion is an everlasting dominion,
Which shall not pass away,
And His kingdom the one
Which shall not be destroyed. (Dan 7:13-14 NKJV)

This passage would have been known by virtually all Jews in Jesus' time. The Son of Man was the Messiah, who would receive power and dominion. When the Samaritan woman at the well told Jesus that people were waiting for the Messiah, Jesus unequivocally answered, "I am he." The Messiah was a man, but a man like no other, who would come to the Father (the Ancient of Days) and be given an eternal Kingdom—which is the re-creation and fulfillment of the Trinity's eternal plan.

A Dividing Line

In light of Christ's eternal, cosmic existence as the Second Person of the Trinity, it is all too easy to downplay the significance of his humanity. The Apostle John saw this as a dividing line between authentic and errant Christianity.

> *This is how you can know God's Spirit: Every spirit who confesses that Jesus Christ came to earth as a human is from God, and every spirit that does not confess Jesus is not from God. (1 Jn 4:2-3)*

We know that Jesus came as a human and lived fully in that condition: He was hungry, he got tired, he felt sadness, joy and even indignation. He had to deal with disappointments, distractions and delays—just like us. The writer of Hebrews said that Jesus had to learn obedience by the things that he suffered. Surely, this learning was taking place for years before the Cross.

> *For we do not have a high priest who is unable to empathize with our weaknesses, but we have one who has been tempted in every way, just as we are—yet he did not sin. (Heb 4:15 NIV)*

To help me see Jesus in his human fullness, I often read the Gospel episodes in the second person; instead of reading the narrative in John 4 "He was tired," I participate in the event of Jesus' reality by reading, or even saying out loud, "Jesus, you are tired." To see him in the Gospels as a very real person who does not get a "pass" because he is God, is an important step, moving from the Incarnation as a concept and entering into its reality. Yet conversely, I also read the Gospels to go beyond Jesus' words and actions,

> "to enter in and *pass through the words* (emphasis added) of revelation to establish, by faith, a vital contact with the Christ who dwells in our souls as God."[68]

As we consider his resurrection and ascension, it is important to remember Jesus did not at this point leave his humanity behind, as something no longer needed, as if he completed his mission and now he can move on. No. For all eternity, he is still fully human; in fact, he is the perfect and complete human. He is what the Trinity always planned for all of humanity. Therefore, he is still Jesus of Nazareth, he has a very real resurrected body, he is still a Jewish man, *and* he is the One who is reigning over the universe, holding it together. He became human so that humanity could become like him. He is seated at the right hand of the Father (Mt 26:64; Col 3:1); therefore, humanity is seated there right now. Jesus, as the firstborn from among the dead, is the first of a whole new race of humanity. Paul writes that Christ is the first born of all creation. He is the first of a whole new creation. He not only took on my humanity, he has restored it permanently. At the right hand of the Father, Jesus holds in himself the life that I will have forever, a concrete life, not some kind of ethereal being floating around for eternity. Rather, in my new, re-created body, I am a new creation that is

---

68 Thomas Merton, *New Seeds of Contemplation*, (New Directions Publishing Co., 2008) p.156

being re-created *right now* (2 Cor 5:17), and will continue on this journey for all eternity.

Because in Christ, humanity and Deity are perfectly brought together, the Incarnation brings human life its ultimate dignity. The Incarnation shouts to me that God takes my life seriously; that he is intimately involved and values every part of me; that he doesn't just understand me from the distance of His Deity, but from our common experience of flesh and blood life. It is a knowledge that is both identificational and intimate. Christ as fully Man, at the right hand of the Father, is interceding for me right now that I would not be led into temptation (Mt 6), and that I will, today, live in the reality that I am blessed, chosen and in the Beloved (Eph 1:3-6).

* * *

God has always loved his creation; however, at the Incarnation, when the eternal, infinite One came to earth fully as a person, he became a full participant. When God the Son entered the world, at that moment he hallowed it. He removed all doubt about the beauty, the infinite value, and the holiness of his creation. Not cursed, but blessed. Not in darkness, but in light. Something else changed: he brought with him the full reality of Heaven. He is now the ladder that Jacob saw prophetically long before. From now on, Heaven and earth are inextricably connected. Because the Incarnate One is the "same yesterday, today and forever," this truth never changes; it is independent of my awareness, emotional state or thought processes. Nothing can alter the truth that the Kingdom of God is within me (Lu 17:21 NKJV). The Triune God never steps back, he never turns aside, he never stops being with me. When I feel like my failures, my sins, my weak faith have somehow distanced me from the Holy God, the Incarnation speaks deep inside me: "I am always with you. I am always for you. I will always be with you."

The Incarnation points me to what is perhaps an even more astounding truth: for all eternity, but beginning in this life, he is re-forming me, changing me at the core of my being to become like him. I am not doing it. I am not even trying to help him do it. His very presence is trans-forming me. As Paul wrote,

> *And all of us, with unveiled faces, seeing the glory of the*
> *Lord as though reflected in a mirror, are being transformed*
> *into the same image from one degree of glory to another,*
> *for this comes from the Lord, the Spirit. (2 Cor 3:18)*

The Greek word for transformed, *metaschematizo*, actually means transfigured. The same word is used of Christ when he was on Mount Tabor. It is something marvelous, almost exuberant. Jesus is not improving me, getting rid of the rough spots. He is making me into something and someone entirely new. My humanity is in the fullest all-embracing sense, spiritual and physical. At the Incarnation, Christ has redeemed all of me. I do not need to deny any part of me: my sexuality, my emotions, my fears, my failures. At his Incarnation, Jesus has reached across time and embraced *all* of me, comforting and unconditionally accepting every part of me. His embrace not only heals me, it slowly transfigures me. I am in him. He is in me, "closer to me than I am to myself."

CHAPTER 5

The Incarnation, Part Two

The Nativity

"How shall man pass into God, unless God has first passed into man? How was mankind to escape death unless he were born again through faith, by that new birth from the Virgin?" St. Irenaeus

Christ was present before and beyond the dimensions of time and space; he was the Creator of the universe; he was interacting with Israel throughout the Old Testament. But there came a specific moment in time two thousand years ago when Christ, the creator of all, entered his creation and became a full member with it. All considerations of Christ's humanity must begin with his virgin birth, for this was where the Word became flesh.

It is vital that we look beyond the romanticized images of Jesus' birth with which most of us grew up. What took place in the Nativity stands at the center of the mystery of Christ, a mystery that is shrouded in the ordinary. To see God in a cave, lying in a feeding trough is to begin to recognize him everywhere. The Nativity is the place where heaven and earth intersect, where God and man become one, uniting us with him forever. In the Nativity we see the depth of God's engagement with us. He has always been "the Lord, the Lord, full of mercy" but now he moves beyond compassion to full participation with his creation. Through his participation we are given an empowering model that challenges us to never distance ourselves from our pain, distress or suffering—or that of the world around us—because fully and without reservation, Jesus entered into our human condition as a human.

Basic to all the creeds, Jesus Christ was conceived by the Holy Spirit and born of a virgin. In the virgin birth the Incarnation has taken on a concrete embodiment. And, as we have seen, this is a whole new life form; this is true Man according to the unwavering purpose of God. In the Nativity God is, at a specific moment in time, at a specific place, re-creating our humanity. In the first creation, God created out of nothing material (*ex nihilo*); now, in the midst of ordinary human life, he is creating in a new way. T.F. Torrance has pointed out that the Nativity and the resurrection stand as twin signs which mark out the mystery of Christ. Jesus was born from the virgin womb of Mary, and was placed in a virgin tomb "where no one had ever been laid."[69]

In reaction to what much of the Protestant church saw (mistakenly, I believe) in the Catholic church as worshiping Mary, there has for several hundred years been somewhat of a downplaying of her role in the Incarnation. It is true that Mary was a simple teenaged girl from the servant class, who was willing to say 'yes' to the angel. But to stop at this is to overlook that she was

---

69   T.F. Torrance, *Incarnation*, p.96

uniquely "blessed among women," and that the Triune God chose her from all women throughout time. From the earliest days of the church, Mary was honored (not worshiped) as the *Theotokos*, that is "God-bearer"—the title that the liturgical church around the world gives to Mary. Jesus was fully human only because he was born of Mary. The church fathers saw Mary prefigured in the Old Testament; for them, the Ark of the Covenant held the presence of God which pointed prophetically to Mary who held the Incarnate Christ. St. Irenaeus understood Mary's obedience and faith as the key to making the re-creation possible.

> "The knot of Eve's disobedience was loosed by the obedience of Mary. For what the virgin Eve had bound fast through unbelief, this did the virgin Mary set free through faith."[70]

Mary responded to the angel, "Behold the maidservant of the Lord. Let it be to me according to your word." This was the critical moment in all of human history, because God would not violate his gift of free will. Mary had a choice, and what she chose changed everything.

As always, there are levels of meaning to be found in all of Scripture and the Nativity account is no exception. St. Augustine saw this in the manger where the animals find their food; but now, lying in the manger, is he who called himself the true Bread come down from heaven, the true nourishment that we need in order to be fully ourselves. This is the Bread that gives us true life, eternal

---

70   St. Irenaeus, *Against Heresies*, III. 322

life. Therefore, the manger becomes the table of God to which we are invited so as to receive the bread of God.[71] An elaborate icon from the 13th century connects the Nativity and the Crucifixion. The Baby is wrapped in swaddling clothes that clearly prefigure the grave clothes in which he would be wrapped following his Crucifixion.[72]

As we will continue to see, the mystery of Christ is filled with paradox, and the Nativity reveals that this was always true. The Incarnation is clothed in hiddenness: a seemingly insignificant girl caught in a socially embarrassing situation; a poor couple arriving in a small town without anywhere to stay; a birth taking place in a cave set aside for cattle. And yet in the midst of this hiddenness, heaven cannot contain itself, shouting out to the shepherds and the world,

"Glory to God in the highest!"

We see the kenotic, self-emptying, movement of God: first, the self-emptying humility that leads Christ downward, followed by his exaltation to the right hand of the Father. This is what, in her song, known as the Magnificat, Mary prophesied about life in the new reality that Jesus would call the Kingdom of heaven:

He has brought down the powerful from their thrones and lifted up the lowly; he has filled the hungry with good things and sent the rich away empty. (Lu 1:52-53)

71　Joseph Ratzinger citing St Augustine on John 6, (Ignatius Press, 2002)

72　https://antiochianprodsa.blob.core.windows.net/ websiteattachments/Nativity%20Icon%20-%20FR%20Kfouf.pdf

The Incarnation shouts a new reality. The way up is the way down. The movement of God will begin with the smallness of a mustard seed ... but it will grow and grow.

The Nativity reminds me not to resist the low way, not to be discouraged when I feel invisible. It reminds me that, no matter how hidden away I think I am, Jesus is always at work. As Paul wrote to the Ephesians, regardless of how I feel or what my circumstances seem to be, I am blessed; I am chosen; I am hidden in the Beloved (Eph 1:3-6).

If we embrace the paradox that is found in the Nativity, the heart of the Incarnation, it will both confront and comfort us. The Nativity reminds us that Christ comes to us in surprising and unexpected ways, which so often contradict our assumptions of what he is doing or what he *should* be doing. It invites us, in the words of Thomas Keating, "to consent and surrender to the Ultimate Mystery just as he is, not as we think he is."

Here lies the beauty of the Nativity narrative. It points to the great and all-embracing truth that the depth, the sheer beauty of Christ and his work in creation is revealed in the ordinary. Because of the Incarnation, everything is new, although often hidden. The Incarnate Christ, who is always at work re-creating, calls me to a journey of trust, believing that his presence, even when I feel nothing, is forming me. The Creator never stops creating me. The Lover never stops loving me.

The Cross

We will consider the mystery of the Cross more fully at a later time, but a brief discussion at this point will help us to see the incarnational connection between the Nativity and the Cross—by which we mean the passion, crucifixion, descent into Hades, and the resurrection. Whether we believe that Jesus came to earth to redeem mankind from the tragic effects of the Fall, or that he came to point us back to the love of the Father, in either case at the heart of his mission was reconciliation, which is defined as: *to restore relations between, or to cause to coexist in harmony.* At the Cross Jesus was victorious over the power of sin, Satan, and death, setting us free to live in unbroken fellowship with the Father. What began at the Nativity came to completion at the Cross.

The fullest revelation of God is Christ on the Cross. It is the culmination of his kenotic love, the same love that was poured out in creating the cosmos. Jesus emptied himself completely, as Paul writes, "even to death on a cross." He entered creation, knowing that he would suffer because of its fallenness. Jesus Christ created and he is still creating. He suffered and is still suffering. The Incarnation and the Cross tell me that Jesus is still identifying and participating in the suffering that is going on right now in the world. At the Cross, Jesus suffered to the full. What he accomplished there, he declared finished. Reconciliation and victory were completed for all time. But his suffering was not. As I write this, tens of thousands of innocent people are suffering terribly in Ukraine and Gaza. The Incarnate Christ is not looking on; he is in the midst of his creation, suffering with the people. When Christ came to earth, he embraced all of the human condition. This was and is one of the great costs, the great emptyings, that Jesus Christ paid when he obeyed his Father and became part of his own creation.

We must not think too lightly of Christ's suffering, but neither should we ignore the great victory that he won for his creation over the power of the enemy. The Cross, after all, has a supremely happy ending. The cost of the Incarnation was suffering, but the purpose was to bring us back to the limitless and eternal love of the Father.

St. Isaac stated that God did this so that humanity would know his immeasurable love for everyone, that our hearts would be captivated and transformed as we behold his power and love displayed through the death of his Son.[73]

Paradox

Mysteries can fill our hearts with wonder, moving us from our places of certainty and assumption. This can be deeply unsettling, and it should be. We cannot for very long hold onto both the old paradigms and at the same time, enter into the new. That is why Jesus said that anyone who puts his hand to the plough and then looks back is unable to pursue the reality of the Kingdom. Jesus wasn't judging; he was stating a truth. As James wrote, "A double-minded man is unstable in all his ways." When we pursue the mystery of Christ, we are stepping into a land filled with paradox. Nowhere is this more true than when we consider the Incarnation.

---

73   Hilarion Afeyev, *The Spiritual World of Isaac the Syrian,* (Cistercian Publications, 2000) p.52

Paul addressed the paradox of the Gospel when he wrote

We proclaim Christ crucified, a stumbling block to Jews and foolishness to gentiles, but to those who are the called, both Jews and Greeks, Christ the power of God and the wisdom of God. For God's foolishness is wiser than human wisdom, and God's weakness is stronger than human strength. (1 Cor 1:23-25)

John Behr refers to this mysterious wisdom of God as "the coincidence of opposites." This was a constant throughout Christ's ministry. Like us when facing the unexpected, the religious leaders' certainties were shaken by these opposites. Jesus spoke with authority, but did not operate within the bounds of what they considered proper for a teacher. Gregory of Nazianzen highlights some of the paradoxes that Jesus lived within.

"As a man he was baptized, but as God he washed away our sins. He had no need of purification, but he wished to sanctify the waters. As a man he was tempted, but as God he triumphed ... He was hungry, but he fed thousands and he is 'the living bread which came down from heaven.' He was thirsty, but he cried, 'If anyone thirsts, let him come to Me and drink' ... he knew weariness, but he is the rest for 'all who labor and are heavy laden.' He asks where Lazarus has been laid, for he is a man; but he raises him to life, for he is God ... he was weak and wounded, but he cures all infirmity and all weakness ... he dies, but he brings to life, and by his own death destroys death."[74]

----

74   Olivier Clement, *Roots of Christian Mysticism*, p.43

The great paradox is that Jesus Christ is fully human and at the same time, fully God. With this as the foundational truth, we should look for him in the midst of contradictions, of seeming opposites. Contemplating the Incarnation compels us to step back from the black-and-white, in-or-out, right-or-wrong dualism of our framework for understanding Christ, the Gospel, others, and even ourselves.

The Church and the Incarnation

Both Paul and John expressed the church's identity in light of the Incarnation in very concrete terms. For Paul, the church was the body of Christ; for John, it was the bride. Both of these terms are often presented as metaphors to help us understand the relationship between Christ and his church, rather than expressions of her true identity. This is regrettable because it reduces the power of what Paul called a great mystery.

> *For this reason a man will leave his father and mother and be joined to his wife, and the two will become one flesh. This is a great mystery, but I am speaking about Christ and the church. (Eph 5:31-32)*

Paul is suggesting that marriage was created by God *because* the Church is Christ's body and bride. The "one flesh" of marriage was created by God from the beginning to prefigure the union of Christ and the church,

> "The apostle's aim was not amiss when he compared the first condition of Adam with that of Christ. ...

For her sake the Word left his Father in heaven …
he came down to be bonded with this woman, the
church."[75]

Just as Adam was only complete when Eve was created, so Christ is completed by the Church.

To better understand the Incarnation, we need to contemplate the Church quite literally as the body and bride of Christ. How amazing that Paul would say the church is actually one flesh with Christ. Surely this takes us beyond being his representatives on earth. When Paul speaks of the body of Christ, he is not using a poetic phrase that sounds nice to describe the church. He is convinced that the Church is the real and organic expression and presence of Christ.

The Church is not an organization; she has no true life apart from him. Rather, she is a living organism, with Christ's very life in her midst as he builds her up by the presence and power of his Spirit. She is not only a beacon, pointing to Christ; she is one with him. Christ manifests his life through her.

"Thus the church has no independent existence, as if it were anything at all or has any life or power of its own, apart from what is unceasingly communicated to it through its union and communion with Christ who dwells in it by the power of the Spirit and fills it with the eternal life and love of God himself."[76]

---

75   Methodius, *Catena Bible*

76   T.F. Torrance, *Theology in Reconstruction*, p.205. Cited by Marcus
     Johnson (Center for Pastor Theologians, Dec. 17, 2020)

The living presence of Christ indwells what he alone has created. From the beginning, Jesus promised that wherever people gather because of him, he is there. This is not an ethereal presence. Jesus Christ is physically in his Church. Just as he physically entered the world as a Man, Christ has entered the Church. Anything less (which I fear we settle for) would not be incarnational and therefore saving, because his Incarnation is always about salvation—reconciling and re-creating into something entirely new.

With the understanding that the incarnate Christ is physically present in the Church, a new awareness as sacred space grows within us. Contemplating the depths of meaning in the Incarnation will inevitably lead us to take the eucharistic sacrament more seriously. Though Christ is always with us, there is a vital renewal of body and spirit that takes place through the elements of the bread and wine. The Lord's Supper proclaims our salvation in its fullest sense, past, present and future: it declares the *past* saving work of the Cross; the *present* reality of Christ's indwelling presence; and the *future* greatly anticipated truth of Jesus' coming again when everything will be made new for all time. For this reason I am convinced that the Lord's Supper is much more than a memorial to what Christ did. It is part of his mysterious re-creation of all things. Not only do we approach worship with a new sense of his holy presence with us, we recognize at a deeper level that we carry his presence with us outside the walls of our gatherings.

For John, the church is being prepared and perfected as a bride for Jesus Christ. For Paul, the mystery that the church is the ongoing expression and reality of the one-flesh union with Christ caused him to write one of the most amazing truths in Scripture:

> *And he has put all things under his feet and has made him the head over all things for the church, which is his body, the fullness of him who fills all in all. (Eph 1:22-23)*

According to Paul, we are the fullness of Christ and are being continually filled by him in a constant, dynamic relationship. The eternal Church is holy ground indeed.

The great destiny of the Church is bound up in her purpose: that Christ might both have, and present to his Father, a glorious Bride, and thus be fully united on the Day when he returns. This is the "summing up of all things in Christ" as recorded by John.

> *Then I heard what seemed to be the voice of a great multitude, like the sound of many waters and like the sound of mighty thunderpeals, crying out, "Hallelujah! For the Lord God the Almighty reigns. Let us rejoice and exult and give him the glory,*
> *For the marriage of the Lamb has come, and his bride has made herself ready. (Rev 19:6-7)*

This great multitude is filled with praise because the time has come at last for the Lamb of God to be joined to his people. This union is so complete that it can only be compared to the marriage of a man and a woman. In first century Israel the wedding took place in two segments. The first, the betrothal, was a covenant commitment. In the New Testament, the Church is presented as the fiancé to Jesus, awaiting the day of marriage. She is betrothed to

Christ by faith. In the second stage, the actual wedding reaches its climax with the wedding supper. For the church, this is the final union with Christ at his second coming. On that great day, the entire cosmos will see the Church for what she really is: the precious bride of Jesus. Jesus' first miracle at the wedding feast of Cana was a prophetic sign, finding its culmination at the wedding supper of the Lamb.

When we are confronted with the Church's weakness and failings, we must hold onto this greater, ultimate truth. Though she is often looked down upon now, her final destiny is certain. As the famous 19th century preacher Charles Spurgeon wrote:

> "The Bride of Christ is a sort of Cinderella now, sitting among the ashes. She is like her Lord, 'despised and rejected of men'; the watchmen smite her, and take away her veil from her; for they know her not, even as they knew not her Lord. But when he shall appear, then shall she appear also, and in his glorious manifestation she also shall shine forth as the sun in the kingdom of the Father."[77]

Our great tendency is to live and perceive within the limitations of the temporal, and so to miss the eternal workings of God. This is why Paul insists that we must always remember that we are people of the Spirit, that we are seated with Christ in heavenly places (Eph 2:6). As we hold onto this truth, we are able to see with the eyes of faith the great and glorious mystery of God's purpose and plan for Christ and the church.

---

77   Charles Spurgeon, *The Marriage of the Lamb*, 1889, (https://www.spurgeon.org/resource-library/sermons/the-marriage-of-the-lamb)

What is the Significance of the Incarnation?

As already noted, the subject of the Incarnation is so centrally important that it is difficult to establish the boundaries of any discussion. However, it may be best to conclude with some overarching points to help bring clarity as to why the study and contemplation of the Incarnation can open up new vistas on our journey.

First of all, it is vital that we absorb this truth: Jesus Christ is the full revelation of God. He is not just one facet of God. God did not become Christlike; this is who he has been from all eternity. Whenever we are unsure or insecure about what God is like, we need to remember and meditate upon this. There is no aspect of the Triune God that is not revealed in who Christ is. He is exactly like the Father. Exactly. The Incarnation means that the eternal Triune relationship has now come to earth.

I have stressed this because I am convinced that much of 21st century evangelicalism has missed this truth. Jesus did not come as the Father's representative. He is the "exact expression" and full revelation of the Father. He did not come as a smaller or junior version of God. We have imagined too small a Christ. And a smaller Christ means a smaller Gospel. As Bradley Jersak has written, "Jesus is the decisive revelation of who God is and the radical re-definition of what God is like."[78]

Because Jesus Christ is the exact expression of the Father, he is the only one who could reveal the true character of the Father to the world. Just like in our day,

---

78 Bradley Jersak, *A More Christlike God*, (Plain Truth Ministries, 2016) np

for the Jews, the Father was often seen primarily as a judge. However, Jesus came to help us to better see the Father. John stresses this truth throughout his Gospel: "I and the Father are One." "If you've seen Me, you've seen the Father." Jesus is exactly like the Father.

The way that God came to earth is a revelation of his true nature. The way the Triune God rules the cosmos is exactly like how Jesus of Nazareth lived. This is critical. *How* he came reveals God's true nature. At the Cross, Jesus defeated the Powers That Be, but in a most surprising way. He did it by refusing to fight back, by emptying himself, just as he had been doing throughout his whole life. Look for self-emptying, kenotic love and you will see Jesus. Kenotic love is both the highest revelation of who God is and the greatest power in the universe.

The Incarnation is counter-intuitive. To this day, like the first century Jews, it is all too easy to be on the lookout for a warrior king. We are seeking the Lion of the Tribe of Judah, but when we find him, we discover he is a slain Lamb (Rev 5:5-6). This is how the Incarnation began; this is who Christ will always be.

Since man could not come to God, God took the initiative and came to man. Therefore, the Incarnation is God's greatest act of deliverance, restoring us to communion with him. St Irenaeus stated: "For this is why the Word became man, and the Son of God became the Son of man: so that man, by entering into communion with the Word and thus receiving divine sonship, might become a son of God."[79]

79　Irenaeus, *Against Heresies*, (Hendrickson Pub, Vol I, 2012) p.448

Jesus' life and teaching were more than a model for how to truly live. His life points forward to God's ultimate purpose: the restoration of all things, that heaven and earth become one. Jesus came as a new humanity and is, therefore, the forerunner for all of us.

Christ not only identifies, he participates in what *we* are and in what we experience so that we can share in *his* life and all who he is. He shares in our death so that we can share in his life. Jesus Christ is the meeting point of God and man in all of the cosmos. He is the point in time and space where divinity and humanity connect.

Because fully God became fully man, human life has great intrinsic value, which comes from the image of God that we *all* bear. This understanding of Christ in everyone shatters the prejudices and false assumptions that lead to so much pain and destruction. This is how to overcome evil with good, to love our enemies, to pursue true understanding with people and cultures that seem so different from us. I believe that one of his greatest re-creating works is for us to gradually learn to see Christ in everyone, even the most "un-Christlike." Surely this is part of Jesus' oft-repeated directives to all who will follow his way: "He who loses his life will find it." Because of the Incarnation, I can see God as he truly is. When I take time to contemplate his true identity, like Paul, I am transformed from glory to glory (2 Cor 3:18). Through this transformation I am progressively conformed into the image of God's Son (Ro 8:29). I enter the journey of seeing Jesus everywhere and in everyone. This is the power of incarnational life—Christ in me, the hope of glory.

When the Word became flesh, God could never again be understood as an abstract, distant, or faceless Deity.

The Incarnation beckons me into intimacy with him. Because of the Incarnation I can settle for nothing less than deeply knowing him.

The Incarnation is the eternal union of Man and God. For all eternity, the Son of God, the Son of Man, the second Person of the Trinity is one of us. He became human; he will remain human. Jesus entered into our fallen existence. The Eternal One, in all his purity, joy, righteousness and omnipotence, knew fully what it was to experience fatigue, hunger, limitations, brokenness, fear, and death. Without the Incarnation, God could look upon our condition with compassion, but in the Incarnation, Jesus immersed himself in our alienation and darkness, yet he never yielded to them. Light conquered darkness (Jn 1:5). He refused to live his life as anything but the Son of God. This is why the Apostle Paul calls Christ "the last Adam." While Adam yielded to the temptation to be like God, knowing good and evil, the last Adam *was God who became man* in order to triumph over the very powers and temptations that defeated the first Adam. Though tempted in his humanity, he never yielded to it. St. Cyril eloquently stated:

> "The common element of humanity is summed up in his person, which is also why he was called the last Adam; he enriched our common nature with everything conducive to joy and glory just as the first Adam impoverished it with everything bringing corruptions and gloom."[80]

80　St. Cyril, *Ancient Christian Commentary*, Vol IV (IVP Academic, 2003) p.145

In the mystery of the Incarnation—this perfect union of man and God—lies an infinitely deep and beautiful truth, one worthy of a lifetime of meditation and adoration. This is the beauty of God revealed. This is the beauty that reconciles the whole cosmos.

* * *

The Incarnation invites me into mystery and as we have seen, mysteries by their very nature are marked by paradox. It is these that can lead me into times of confusion, uncertainty, discouragement and sometimes even anger. However, if I don't let go, if I don't give up, it is these very paradoxes that Christ most uses for my growth. God is love; his mercies endure forever. Those are bedrock truths for me. But they do not protect me from the reality of suffering (both manmade and natural), of tragedy, of conflict. "Pain is the rent we pay for being human."[81]

One of the Incarnation's greatest mysteries is that the Infinite One, the Creator of all, embraced such smallness and hiddenness, becoming an infant born in a cave in a small town. This turns me away from the big and beautiful, the successful and influential; instead it tells me that beauty is revealed in the ordinary. When I let this truth sink in, sometimes it leads me to look at and appreciate all of the small and hidden things around me. Sometimes it causes me to leave my "achievement" orientation and to simply slow down, even stop for that one object, that one situation, that one person. Sometimes.

---

81 Richard Rohr, *Solidarity With Pain*, (Center for Action and Contemplation, Sept 9, 2016)

The Incarnation shouts to us that all lives have great value, because all of life is made in the image of God. His essence—which is perfect love—is in the fabric of the entire cosmos. This is one of the most important truths for me to contemplate; for several years it has led to an ongoing shift in how I see the natural world. It is not fallen or evil; it is good, because God declared it so from the very beginning. Creation is an indescribably good gift from our Father (Jas 1:17). This is why, especially as those who purpose to follow the Jesus Way, we must be protectors of the earth. Matter is not neutral. It is God-breathed. Creation is not God, but it is a reflection of who God is. It is a means by which he reveals himself to us. We cannot care for the galaxies, but we *can* care for our cities, our nations. In doing so we honor our Creator..

If I am going to be honest in my journey into the mystery of Christ, then I must let Jesus' suffering also change me. As he emptied himself in both trusting obedience to his Father and great compassion for us, he suffered more and more. The truth of getting close to Jesus, what he calls abiding in him, is that in the process I receive a greater alignment with his heart for humanity. This means more heart-suffering. It means pain for all those who live in the suffering of war, famine, and natural disaster. I feel the pain of these more than I used to. I think this is because I am getting closer to the One who holds all suffering in his heart.

The Incarnation was not a change; it was a whole new beginning, a re-forming, a new creation without limits. "Behold, I make all things new!", including me.

CHAPTER 6

Established in His Humanity

Throughout his life and ministry, the mystery of Christ's perfect union of God and man continually challenged all those who encountered him, even including his own family. They saw a very human man among them, and yet, One upon whom heaven seemed to break in repeatedly, resulting in human actions that were somehow beyond human. Conversely, as Jesus himself proclaimed his unique divinity as the Son of God, his humanity made this very hard for so many to receive. Surely God wouldn't look or act like this.

Having established Jesus Christ's hypostatic union—fully God and fully man—an overview of his ministry in Israel may help us to see the intrinsic mystery contained and revealed in all that he did. This is a huge topic, so we will limit ourselves to highlighting a few episodes.

Jesus as a Boy

Luke gives us the only recorded incident about Jesus' youth and the only one between his infancy and the beginning of his ministry. Since the New Testament tells us that if all the things that Jesus did and taught were written down, "even the whole world could not contain them" (Jn 21:25), it is always important to consider, why is *this* episode included?

At the end of the Nativity chapter (Luke 2), it is significant that we encounter Jesus here as a child; in fact Luke is deliberately taking us into Jesus' journey from child to young man. It helps us to perceive the greater significance of this episode in the Temple if we remember that Jesus did not enter the world as an adult; he came as a child. There is a sense in which Jesus never loses childlike qualities. George MacDonald develops this beautifully in *Creation in Christ*. Just as Jesus expresses the Father, the child expresses Jesus.

> *So whoever will humble himself like this child, he is the greatest in the kingdom of heaven. And whoever receives one such child in My name, receives Me. (Mt 18:4-5 NASB)*

The Triune God is represented in the child. MacDonald insists that childhood belongs to this divine nature. No wonder that Jesus, the full revelation of God welcomes, includes, and embraces the little children. In his purity, devotion, and trust, Jesus is child-like. And this is the way that the Incarnate One has made for us.

> *"Truly I tell you, whoever does not receive the kingdom of God as a little child will never enter it." (Mk 10:15)*

This is the second time that Jesus has come to Jerusalem; it is the Passover feast, which years later will find its final fulfillment in him. At a literal level, Jesus had come to the time in life when a boy began to enter manhood. Mary and Joseph were meeting the requirements of the law, bringing Jesus to his confirmation. He would no longer receive instruction on the law through his parents; now Jesus would take that responsibility upon himself, learning from the priests and scribes.

Jesus was being obedient to both his parents and his heavenly Father. There is something mysterious in Jesus' response: "Did you not know that I must be in My Father's house?" This can equally be translated, "I must be about my Father's business." For anyone to refer to God as Father would have been almost scandalous; how much more so to be uttered by a twelve year old boy? St. Bede saw in this episode a revealing of Jesus' dual nature as God and man.

> "When he was sitting in the temple, the Lord said, 'I must be about my Father's business,' and this is a declaration of his power and glory which are co-eternal with God the Father's. However, when he returned to Nazareth, he was subject to his parents, and this is an indication of his true humanity as well as an example of humility."[82]

We see Jesus' human identity revealed in that he humbly listened to the religious teachers, but as God, he spoke with divine wisdom, what James calls the "wisdom from above." (Jas 3:17) As St Cyril wrote, "He is filled with wisdom who is Himself all wisdom."[83] This is why the teachers were amazed. This was not just a very clever

---

82 St. Bede, *Ancient Christian Commentary on Scripture, NT, Vol 3* (InterVarsity Press, 2003) p.55

83 St. Cyril, *Commentary on the Gospel of Luke, Sermon V,* (https:// www.ecatholic2000.com/cyril/untitled-07.shtml)

and gifted boy; they recognized that something else was at work, something beyond merely human. We see in this incident that Jesus was responsible to both his Father and to his parents, but his first responsibility was to his Father. This never changed. Years later, Jesus would say that he only did what he saw the Father doing (Jn 5:19). However, he lived out that obedience in the context of complete submission to Mary and Joseph.

The boy Jesus was fully the Son of God, and yet he remained obedient and in subjection as a son to his earthly parents. As T.F. Torrance points out, by living in earthly obedience to Mary and Joseph, Jesus lived as the Son of Man and opened up a way for all of us by making humanity itself the Father's house. His obedience was the way in which "Jesus increased in wisdom and in stature, and in favor with God and man." (Lu 2:52) From the beginning, his obedience was costly, which Luke made clear by translating "increased" with the Greek word *prokopto*, which means to forcefully drive forward as if by beating.[84] From the beginning, Jesus' obedience involved a battle. To learn to look deeper, beyond the literal or surface meaning, will take us closer to the incredible struggles and the cosmic stakes that were constantly a part of his life.

Jesus' obedience flowed from his humility. As Paul tells us

> *And when he had come as a man,*
> *he humbled himself by becoming obedient*
> *to the point of death —*
> *even to death on a cross. (Phil 2:7-8)*

---

84   Strong's Greek Dictionary #4298

Like obedience, his humility was learned and lived out from a young age and it marked his life as the Son of Man. He told us to learn from him for he is gentle and humble in heart. St. Isaac wrote:

"Humility is the ornament of the Godhead. The Word clothed himself in it when He became man. By it He lived among us in the flesh ... And anyone who wraps himself in it truly makes himself like Him who came down from on high and clothed his grandeur and glory in humility."[85]

As we seek to grow in grace, it is a comfort and encouragement to know that, albeit imperfectly, we are following the One who, childlike, obedient, and humble, went before us and who continues to empower us as we fix our eyes on him, the author and finisher of our faith (Heb 12:1-2).

From early days, the church fathers recognized at least two more points of mystery in this narrative. Jesus was at the Temple in Jerusalem for three days before his parents returned and found him. St. Ambrose says that this was not because of Mary and Joseph's forgetfulness, nor Jesus'. Rather, it was a prophetic sign that "he who was believed dead for our faith would rise again after three days ... and appear on his heavenly throne with divine honor."[86]

At the end of this episode, Luke writes, "And his mother stored all these things in her heart." (Lu 2:51) St. Bede observed that Mary,

---

85   Isaac the Syrian, cited by Olivier Clement, *The Roots of Christian Mysticism* (New City Press, 1995) p.154

86   St. Ambrose, *Ancient Christian Commentary on Scripture*, NT, Vol 3, p.54

"learned from Jesus, not as from a child or man, but as from God. Yes, she dwelt in meditation on his words and actions. Nothing of what was said or done by him fell idly on her mind. As before, when she conceived the Word itself in her womb, so now does she hold within her his ways and words ... That which she now beholds in the present, she waits to have revealed with greater clarity in the future."[87]

Mary holds within her the deep, years-long contemplation of the mystery of Christ—her son and her Lord—his hypostatic union, the present and future mingling and reflecting each other, and his cosmic authority paradoxically expressed through his self-emptying.

The Baptism of Jesus

The ministry of Jesus now begins. As always, we are faced with depths of meaning. In his baptism we see death and resurrection, identification and confrontation with the sin of humanity; the direct involvement of the Trinity; and the fulfillment of Old Testament signs.

The centrality of his baptism is evident in that all four Gospels record it; as well, six epistles teach about baptism as the foundation and initiation of the Christian faith.

Why was Jesus the Son of God baptized? Even John the Baptist was amazed that Jesus asked for this. When John said, "I should be baptized by you" he was saying, "I am just a man; you are the Messiah, the Son of God. I am a sinner; You are without sin." Yet Jesus responds,

---

87 St. Bede. *Ancient Christian Commentary on Scripture*, p.55

"Let it be so now, for it is proper for us in this way to fulfill all righteousness." (Mt 3:15) John had been proclaiming and activating a baptism of repentance. Jesus was about to bestow a new baptism for the salvation of all humanity. Our salvation, our life with Christ connects us with him at his baptism. This is a central theme for Paul. Nowhere does he state this more clearly than in Romans 6:4

> *Therefore we were buried with him by baptism into death, so that, just as Christ was raised from the dead by the glory of the Father, so we also might walk in newness of life.*

And this is a dimension of the mystery: somehow, beyond the constraints of different times and places, we are present with Christ in his baptism, immersed in his death and raised up into his resurrection life.

St. Maximus sees another aspect of Jesus' fulfilling all righteousness.

"What sort of baptism is this of the Savior, I ask, in which the streams are made pure more than they purify? ... Since the Savior plunged into the waters, he sanctified the outpouring of every flood and course of every stream by the mystery of his baptism ... When someone wishes to be baptized in the name of the Lord, it is not so much the water of this world that covers him but the water of Christ that purifies him. Yet the Savior willed to be baptized for this reason—not that he might cleanse himself but that he might cleanse the waters for our sake."[88]

---

88 St. Maximus, *Ancient Christian Commentary on Scripture, NT Vol III,* p.67

In a mysterious way, creation itself was made holy through Christ's baptism.

Jesus fulfilled all righteousness by humbly entering the ranks of sinners and acting on their behalf. It is significant that Jesus was baptized along with what was likely a large crowd on the banks of the Jordan, waiting his turn like everyone else. He did not set himself apart but identified fully. Jesus was not baptized for his sin (he had none); rather he was sanctifying the waters of baptism which wash away the sin of all who would enter them.

> "Beginning with his baptism among sinners at the Jordan to fulfill all righteousness, and ending with his baptism in blood on the cross, again among malefactors when he died, the just for the unjust, we see the person of Christ at work in a movement of increasing solidarity with his fellow men and women, increasing solidarity with sinners."[89]

Jesus' baptism was an anticipation of the Cross. He fulfilled all righteousness by not only identifying with humanity, but taking its guilt upon himself and carrying it down into the water. As Paul wrote, "For we died and were buried with Christ by baptism." Jesus' first public act was to step into the place of sinners; this identification would culminate at the Cross.

John's baptism was about repentance; Jesus' baptism was about entering into eternal life—the new beginning—of knowing the Triune God (Jn 17:3). This is why it was so important for Priscilla and Aquila to explain this vital

---

89   T.F. Torrence, *Incarnation*, p.106

distinction to Apollos, who was preaching Christ, but with an incomplete understanding.

> *He began to speak boldly in the synagogue; but when Priscilla and Aquila heard him, they took him aside and explained the Way of God to him more accurately. (Act 18:25-26)*

To understand the immense significance of Jesus' baptism, we must look at it through the lens of history. As we saw in an earlier chapter, types are a great help to our understanding. The Apostle Paul and the Church Fathers insisted that the Old Testament was filled with types that found their fulfillment in Christ's baptism. Paul tells the Corinthians that when the Israelites passed through the Red Sea, they were experiencing a type of baptism. St. Chromatius points out the historical link with Israel crossing the Jordan River.

> "Just as it was for the people of that time who made their way into the promised land … with the Lord going before them so now, through the very same waters of the river Jordan, the first path of the heavenly way has been opened up along which we are led to that blessed land of promise … Joshua the son of Nun was their leader; but for us Jesus Christ the Lord stands— through baptism—the leader of eternal salvation."[90]

Gregory of Nyssa illuminates many more Old Testament passages that looked ahead to Christian

---

90   St. Chromatius, *The Church Bible, Matthew,* (Wm. B. Eerdmans Publishing, 2018) p.48

baptism, including Hagar as she and her son Ishmael were about to perish from thirst in the desert, when suddenly Christ appears and shows her a well of living water. Certain death becomes life. Gregory points to many other examples, including Jacob at the well, Elijah pouring water on the sacrifice at Mount Carmel and so on, yet as Gregory wrote:

> "But here we must make an end of the testimonies from the Divine Scriptures: for the discourse would extend to an infinite length if one should seek to select every passage in detail, and set them forth in a single book."[91]

In Christ's baptism, we see again both obedience and humility. Jesus would have walked about 70 miles from Galilee to come to where John was baptizing. Obedience continues to have a cost for Jesus. He took seriously the moment of his baptism. It is also interesting that in John the Baptist's response, we also see *his* humility. At this point, huge crowds were following John. God's favor was clearly on him, but he was not influenced by the adulation. Jesus' baptism was a watershed for John; it was from this time onward that his influence and popularity began to decrease, something he surely anticipated but with which he was content.

In the Scriptures, a mystery is something that is revealed by God in his perfect time. Jesus' baptism was just such a time.

---

91   Philip Schaff citing St. Gregory of Nyssa, *On the Baptism of Christ* (https://www.ccel.org/ccel/schaff/npnf205.xii.iii.html)

*And immediately, coming up from the water, He saw the
heavens parting and the Spirit descending upon Him
like a dove. Then a voice came from heaven, "You are My
beloved Son, in whom I am well pleased."
(Mk 1:10-11 NKJV)*

God the Father has broken his silence and again is
revealing himself to humans. This is a clear sign that the
Messianic Age has begun. He introduces Jesus as the
Son of God. Jesus' ministry begins with this unequivocal
identification and empowerment by the Holy Spirit.
However, his baptism profoundly declares Jesus' identity
as the Son of Man because it reveals his very human need
for affirmation by his Father. He is the Beloved of God;
this is the rock on which his life and ministry will be built.

When the Father declares, "You are *my* beloved Son"
he was meeting Jesus' very human and universal need for
identity and belonging. Jesus knew who he was, and none
of the challenges and attacks that he would face could
ever take that away from him. When the Father called
Jesus "beloved," this established in him an unshakeable
security that set him free to be who he truly was. Because
of this, Jesus was never motivated by any need to justify
himself, or to prove his worth. The unconditional,
unchanging love of the Father was a love that Jesus lived
and remained in; the Father's love for him would, no
matter what, never let go. This opened the door for the
radical risk-taking of true faith. When the Father said, "I
am well pleased with you," he was saying—before Jesus
had engaged in a single day of ministry—that he was
proud of his Son. This commendation gave Jesus a deep

confidence. The Father not only anoints Jesus for service with the Holy Spirit, he also gives him the strengths of identity, security, and confidence. This was the central formative event of Jesus' life and ministry.

Jesus' baptism is perhaps the clearest example of the Trinity being manifested to humanity in the Scriptures. The Father spoke, the Holy Spirit anointed, and Jesus' true identity as the Son of God was revealed. Jesus is the full and perfect revelation of the Triune God; therefore, it is significant that as he is revealed to the world, in the same event, so is the Trinity. Reminiscent of the ark, the Holy Spirit descended like a dove; he must be present at this critical moment because, as St. Ambrose has written, the Trinity can never be separated from itself. The heavens opened to show us the transcendence of what was taking place. Jesus' baptism goes deeper than the event; it was like a bridge, creating a direct connection between the earthly and heavenly realms. In the mystery of Jesus' baptism the Holy Spirit came down and manifested as a dove. The second Person of the Trinity is publicly revealed by the Father as a man. The Holy Spirit is specifically joined together with the Father and Son. The unity of the Trinity is declared and demonstrated. The Father cannot be understood apart from the Son; the Son cannot be known apart from the Holy Spirit. As we consider the baptism of Jesus, we can know that, like him, in our baptism we are united eternally with the Trinity, for the Trinity is our ultimate destiny.

The Temptation in the Wilderness

Then Jesus was led up by the Spirit into the wilderness to be tested by the devil. (Mt 4:1)

This is the first direct conflict that we witness between Christ and Satan. However, as we shall see when we look at Jesus in the Garden, there has been continuous warfare going on. The great overarching mission of Jesus was taking back what Satan had seized, and restoring humanity to its position as guardians of the earth.

For this purpose the Son of God was manifested, that He might destroy the works of the devil. (1 Jn 3:8 NKJV)

Satan is ultimately a defeated foe, but he is not a weak one. John writes that the entire world is under the power of the evil one (1 Jn 5:19) and Paul calls Satan "the god of this world" (2 Cor 4:4). All of Christ's activity is in conflict with Satan. Every healing, deliverance, and repentance is a manifestation of Jesus' advance against the enemy. This is the context for understanding the importance of what took place in the wilderness.

In looking at this episode, we are immediately faced with a question: Who could have told the Gospel writers about what happened? No human witness but Jesus was present. By relaying to them what happened, first of all, he demonstrated his humility. He had been publicly declared as the Son of God, yet he transparently tells the disciples how he was severely tempted. Jesus joined them in their temptations in order to strengthen and help them, and to teach them to walk in the light of truth rather than hide things in shame.

Jesus' temptation begins immediately after his baptism with forty days of fasting in the wilderness, which clearly parallels Israel's forty years of wandering. We may be surprised at the stark contrast from the great honor and empowerment that he has just experienced, but from the beginning, we see the self-emptying kenotic movement of Jesus' life. This time of testing focuses on Jesus' humanity; he becomes both weak and hungry, and this is what Satan uses to tempt him the first time. Yet he faces these temptations fully as a man, *not* as the Son of God. He truly *is* hungry; he doesn't just seem to be. It is striking that although Jesus wouldn't turn stones to bread, he will give his body as bread for all people (Mt 26:26).

Thomas Aquinas gives four clear reasons why the omnipotent Son of God allowed himself to be tempted. Aquinas believes that Jesus *desired* to be tempted so that we might be strengthened against all those temptations that inevitably come against us. Gregory the Great wrote, "It was not unworthy of our Redeemer to wish to be tempted, who came also to be slain; in order that by his temptations He might conquer our temptations just as by his death he overcame our death."[92] Secondly, Christ endured temptation to warn us that no one is ever beyond its reach. If Christ was tempted, so are all of us. Thirdly, Christ endured temptation so that he might be our mediator, One who has been tempted and so entered into the human experience, but never faltered.

---

92   Cited by Steve Jonathan Rummelsburg, *St Thomas Aquinas on Christ's Temptation* (https://catholicexchange.com/st-thomas-aquinas-on-christs-temptation)

Because he himself was tested by what he suffered, he is able to help those who are being tested. (Heb 2:18)

For we do not have a high priest who is unable to sympathize with our weaknesses, but we have one who in every respect has been tested as we are, yet without sin. (Heb 4:15)

Finally, because of his faithfulness in the face of temptation, we have a model for our own victory.

Turning the tables, we may ask what was Satan's motivation for this encounter? Many of the church fathers wrote that the reason Satan confronted Jesus with three temptations was that he was not absolutely certain that Jesus was the Christ; until his baptism, there had been no public indication. So Satan's plan was to entice Jesus into a supernatural act that would confirm his true identity. While we cannot be certain, there is logic in this view.

Jesus had just heard the Father's words of affirmation and identity. It should be no surprise that we see Satan begin by attacking those very words: "If you are the Son of God, turn these stones into bread." It is interesting that these were the same words—If you are the Son of God—thrown at him as he hung on the Cross. Satan always attacks our identity, trying to use doubt as the lever of temptation. In Genesis 3, he uses doubt ("Did God really say?") that leads to the cataclysmic downfall of Adam. Jesus faced Satan as the Son of Man. In his humanity he was the second Adam, the One who never succumbed to doubt.

"It was necessary to defeat the devil, not by God, but by the flesh, for the devil would not have dared to tempt Him unless he recognized the weakness that hunger brings to human nature ... It was fitting that he be defeated by that same humanity in whose death and misfortune he gloried."[93]

Adam left Paradise and went out into the wilderness, "east of Eden"; Jesus goes into the wilderness, in obedience to the Father and the Holy Spirit. This begins to reverse the process of death and alienation, overcoming Satan's deception and therefore beginning to lead us back to Paradise, our true home.

Jesus was so grounded in his identity that nothing could shake him. That is why it is vital that we learn to abide in him, to immerse ourselves in our true identity, the identity that he speaks over us. Our lives are found in him and nothing else.

In the first temptation, Satan tried to work on Jesus' weakness and hunger. Now, in the second, he focuses on Jesus' strength. He never accuses Jesus of not being holy enough; rather, he knows that our strength can be our vulnerability, leading to pride, overconfidence, or presumption. Jesus could throw himself off the pinnacle of the Temple into his Father's arms, but there was no reason to do so. The Father has already validated Jesus at his baptism; to seek another validation would be pre-sumptuous. Here, we see that Jesus gave us a standard for knowing God's will: **Does this honor God? Will it help another person?**

In the third temptation,

______

93   St. Hilary, *Ancient Christian Commentary on Scripture*, Vol 1a NT, p. 57

Again, the devil took him to a very high mountain and showed him all the kingdoms of the world and their glory, and he said to him, "All these I will give you, if you will fall down and worship me." (Mt 4:8-9)

The church fathers are in agreement that this was a vision; there is no literal mountain high enough to see the whole world. The enemy uses our imagination, trying to persuade and delude us. He presents things that are not real and tries to frighten us with things that have not happened as though they have. That is why Paul said to take every thought captive (2 Cor 10:5). Jesus shows us that the enemy's attack, through our thinking and imagination, is both real and powerful.

There is a great irony in this temptation. Satan is offering the possession of the world to the One who created it and the entire cosmos. His temptations are always built upon deception. What makes us so susceptible to his lies is that they feed our broken need to be recognized, to be somehow special apart from the Father's all encompassing blessing. Because Jesus knew in his deepest being who he was, he always spurned the glory of prestige and power. He could not be lured by the ambition of this world. When I contemplate all that took place in the wilderness, I hear a warning. Contrary to all my ambitious desires to be thought well of, I must beware of any offer that feeds my ego-driven need for finding significance and identity apart from my Father's words: "You are my beloved son. I am so pleased with you."

Progressively in these temptations, Satan takes Jesus higher and higher. But the Holy Spirit takes Him lower and lower through his humble obedience of being baptized and then being led to the place of physical weakness and isolation. This is always the way of Christ. What happens in the wilderness where Jesus is confronted by Satan points ahead to the Cross where he defeats Satan, sin and death—not by the power of his divinity, but by the mystery of his humility.

Through the centuries, spiritual leaders and teachers have had much to say about the Temptation in the wilderness. They understood that, as followers of Christ, believers are participating in a great cosmic conflict. St. Isaac insisted that temptation is a sign of God's grace in that battle.

> "A long as you are journeying in the way to the city
> of the Kingdom and are drawing near the city of
> God, let this be for you a signpost: the strength of
> the temptations you encounter. The nearer you draw
> and progress, the more temptations multiply against
> you. Whenever you perceive diverse and intensified
> temptations in your path, therefore, know that at
> that time your soul has in fact secretly entered a new
> higher level, and that grace has been added to her
> in this state where she was found; for God leads the
> soul into the afflictions of trials in exact proportion
> to the magnificence of the grace which he bestows."[94]

It is to be noted that Christ's temptation took place in the desert, not only a place of hardship, but of isolation. Seasons of isolation easily lead us into feelings of

---

94   Hilarion Alfeyev, *The Spiritual World of Isaac the Syrian*, pp. 95-96

abandonment and alienation. This too was part of Satan's assault against Jesus: to entice him into demonstrating that in the desert the Father had abandoned him. This lay behind the temptation to throw himself off the Temple. Feelings of abandonment are universally part of the human experience; there are times when we feel forgotten by people and by God. We are not shielded from these feelings because we are followers of Jesus. The writer to the Hebrews tells us, "let your hearts be established by grace." (Heb 13:9a) This small saying is important for our lives just as it was for Jesus. The central event in Jesus' life was the affirmation he received from the Father at his baptism. This was the bedrock on which his life would stand, no matter what temptations or attacks came his way. Hearts established by grace hear the Father say to them, "I am always with you. I am always for you." (I wrote this in the previous chapter, but the repetition is intentional. We need to hear this again and again.) Feelings of abandonment are just that—feelings. Though our experience may feel like we are separated from God, that is not real; in fact, I do not believe separation is even possible. God does not ever withdraw from a person; it is a subjective experience that he allows in order to renew or create a longing for his presence. Like all of us, St. Isaac knew that feelings of abandonment or alienation could easily lead him to despondency and depression, which he described as being as if his soul was being suffocated. Isaac knew this so strongly that he described it as "a forecast of Gehenna."[95]

---

95   ibid p.103

In Jesus Christ's childhood, baptism, and wilderness temptation, the Father was establishing the final stages of his foundation for ministry.

Through his obedience and humility, with his eyes and heart steadfastly fixed upon his Father, the boy Jesus amazed the religious teachers in the Temple with his understanding. But significantly, he made a way for all of humanity to be with him in the Father's house. When Christ, again in obedience and humility, entered the Jordan River, he opened the way for all of us to be both buried and raised with him in baptism. In a mysterious way, just as he was with me in my baptism, so was I with him in his baptism, unhindered by the bounds of time and space. When Jesus resisted the temptations which tried to challenge his identity, he made a way for me to be, at the core of my being, established in who I truly am in Christ.

* * *

The story of the young Jesus in the Temple sets the stage for an important theme in the Gospels, especially Luke, where he refers to either child or children nearly seventy times. As George MacDonald wrote about at some length, Christ is childlike; therefore it should be no surprise that for Jesus there is something especially sacred about children. He tells us that their angels see the face of the Father in heaven (Mt 18:10); he laid his hands on children, imparting a blessing over their lives; he identified so closely with children that he revealed whoever welcomes a child is welcoming him. It is easy to pass over the importance of Jesus' multiple references to children. Jesus affirmed those who love even their enemies as children of the Father. He insisted that the Father generously gives to children. During his Triumphal Entry, it was the children who cried out, "Hosanna to the Son of David!" If we are surprised by the special place Jesus gives to children, it becomes clearer in Mt 18:3-4

Truly I tell you, unless you change and become like children, you will never enter the kingdom of heaven. Whoever becomes humble like this child is the greatest in the kingdom of heaven.

Jesus is telling us something quite radical, that Christ is represented in the child: humble, vulnerable, transparent. No one would say that this is how children always act; but when they do, when they live from their divine nature, they both reflect and live in the abiding life of Jesus. When he said, "Learn from me for I am gentle and lowly," Jesus was telling us that *he* is childlike. From the time of Constantine when Christianity became the religion of the Empire, we have worshiped, promoted, and looked for the warrior Savior. But the Lamb, the gentle One, is childlike. That is who he is and therefore that is how I am to come to him. Vulnerable, honest, needy, without pretense, without trying to seem stronger, holier, more worthy than I actually am. I take great comfort in knowing that Jesus addressed the paralytic, the lowest person in Jewish society, as "child." (Mt 9:2)

Throughout his life, Jesus overcame not only Satan's temptations, but the duplicity, slander and anger of the religious elite, the rage of mob mentality, and even the incredible forces of sin and death arrayed against him at the Cross. How did he do this? Based on their interpretation of the Old Testament, the Jews were confident that Messiah would come to crush their enemies. (See Psalms 50:3; 89:10; 98:1; 68:12 etc.) The Jews were waiting for a conquering King. Listening to the songs, prayers and rhetoric coming from a large segment of the American church, it seems that very little has changed. But how did Christ overcome and defeat evil: through the gentleness of a child. He absorbed all that came against him, and *he never, not even once, fought back.*

> *Lord when I feel too vulnerable, when I feel in a weak position, when everything in me wants to defend myself, or even strike back through my words or actions—let me remember who You are, my childlike Savior. And once again, let my heart be established by Your grace. Amen.*

CHAPTER 7

Mystery in Ministry

The foundation having been laid, Jesus now embarks upon three years of ministry that will eventually become known throughout the globe. During this whole time, Jesus was demonstrating the mystery of living as both God and Man, the Son who walked in total obedience while also holding the universe together. If we read the Gospels without this awareness, as amazing as his miracles were, we still find ourselves with a Jesus who is too small.

Many of us have only been taught to read the Scriptures at the literal level. As noted earlier, this is a reflection of the rationalism of the Enlightenment, which greatly influenced how the church, especially in the Protestant evangelical tradition, approached Scripture. This literal view assumes that a passage has one correct meaning; this has led to a two-dimensional, largely black-and-white approach to reading Scripture.

The early church fathers taught that every Scripture is to be read in three ways: the literal, moral, and spiritual level. When reading a verse or passage, the literal level is the logical place to start. We begin by asking, "What is the point or truth being conveyed?" Once this has been ascertained, we move on to the moral reading which leads us to look inward, asking ourselves, "How can this truth make me more Christlike?" These two readings are obviously foundational, but the church fathers taught that for reading the passage to be complete, we must press on to the spiritual reading. This has been called the *water-to-wine* reading where we take time to meditate on the passage, letting the Holy Spirit show us something that is new to us, often something that takes us deeper. This is the interpretive dividing line, departing from the constraints of the historical-critical method that bases interpretation upon the author's intent and the way that the original audience would have understood that intent. Reading while being sensitive to the direction of the Holy Spirit may lead us into new spiritual insights, understandings that come from him. We are seeing something by illumination whereby the Holy Spirit directly involves us by means of the Scripture passage. There is no longer one correct, final, reading. What is important is the truth that the Lord brings through the passage. Learning to read the Scriptures this way leads to recognizing the mystery of Christ throughout both Old and New Testaments.

The mystery of Christ is revealed in multifaceted ways throughout the Gospel accounts. We will confine this chapter to a few examples that lead us to a greater sense of mystery, with the hope that this will open us to seeing even more. Clearly, mystery is manifested in the many examples of Jesus' healing—physically, emotionally, and spiritually.

Healings Reveal Mystery

The synoptic Gospel writers, especially Matthew and Mark, grouped a number of healings together. Although they seem to happen in rapid sequence, it is more likely that they were recorded to represent the nature of Jesus' healing ministry. Their rapidity reminds us that, as Jesus told Nathaniel, the activity of heaven is constantly taking place here on earth, and Jesus is the connection between the two realms.

As Jesus walks through a crowd, a woman with an issue of blood reaches out in her desperation and touches the hem of his garment. For years she had been suffering and tried every remedy without success. She represents all of humanity; while we all suffer in many ways, healing comes through Christ. This woman was unclean; no one would come near because of her condition which had gone on for twelve years. Because of this isolation, she was sick physically, emotionally and socially. Jesus *saw* a social outcast, and when he spoke to her, "Have courage daughter, your faith has made you well," she received healing that touched the core of her being. Jesus' power went out to her, in response to her reaching out to him. By healing without her asking, he showed his knowledge of all things. Yet, at other times he had to ask: "What do you need?" "How long have you been like this?" Jesus is Son of God and Son of man. This, too, is part of the mystery. It is also significant that she was likely a Gentile woman from Caesarea Philippi. We know this because there was a statue in that city memorializing this healing event. On different occasions Jesus told the disciples that his ministry was only to the Jews (Mat 10:5-6; 15:24), yet many times he reached beyond that boundary to heal non-Jews, including the Canaanite woman's daughter, the ten Samaritan lepers, and the Centurion. There is something unpredictable about Jesus, and this, too, is part of his mystery. He cannot be confined or categorized.

This encounter with the unclean woman happened while Jesus was on his way to raise the daughter of a religious leader, Jairus, from the dead. When Jesus sent the mourners from the girl's room, declaring, "Go away; for the girl is not dead but sleeping," he was about to reverse death, demonstrating that death would no longer be final. Whereas Jewish law said to never touch a dead body, Jesus took what was dead and made it alive.

Concerning this incident, Chromatius, a fourth century church father, presents us with an outstanding example of water-to-wine interpretation:

> "It is for us to understand that the entire mystery
> of our salvation is prefigured in this girl ... Luke
> reports that Jesus directed the girl to eat something
> ... The order of our faith and salvation is shown
> here. When each believer is freed in baptism from
> perpetual death ('buried and raised with him
> in water baptism') and comes back to life upon
> the acceptance of the gift of the Holy Spirit, it is
> necessary that the person also be directed to eat that
> heavenly bread about which the Lord says, 'Unless
> you eat the flesh of the Son of Man and drink his
> blood, you have no life in you.'"[96]

---

96   Chromatius of Aquileia: *Sermons on the Gospel of Matthew*

Notice his framework of interpretation is mystery. A careful, contemplative reading points both to the depths of Christ and the wonders of our salvation. This is part of the process of being freed from a narrow and trans-actional view of salvation that suggests if we will pray a certain prayer we will go to heaven. In this young girl's being raised we see the miracle of rescue and of mourning turned into joy, prefiguring Christ's resurrection, baptism, and the Eucharist,

Seven hundred and fifty years before Jesus' ministry began, the prophet Isaiah declared that the Messianic Age would be clearly marked by a time when:

> *Then will the eyes of the blind be opened*
> *and the ears of the deaf unstopped.*
> *Then will the lame leap like a deer,*
> *and the mute tongue shout for joy. (Is 35:5-6 NIV)*

The healings, as wonderful as they were (and still are), pointed beyond themselves to something even bigger: there will come a time when all sickness, sin, and even death itself will be no more. Each healing is a prophetic event, revealing the reality of heaven and moving humanity another step closer to that Day when,

> *He will wipe every tear from their eyes.*
> *Death will be no more;*
> *mourning and crying and pain will be no more (Rev 21:4)*

Faith is the Key to healing…or Is It?

On different occasions, Jesus commended faith and even said, "Your faith has made you well." Elsewhere he encouraged the disciples that if they had faith, they could move mountains. And so, we easily conclude that the key to healing is having enough faith—either the person praying or the one receiving. Certainly, there does seem to be a connection between faith and healing. This is an example of how we try to limit the One who is without limits, who is beyond all our boundaries or categories. Decades of pastoring has shown me the harmful effect of this thinking. When someone is suffering and yet not healed, it is all too easy for them (or their church friends and family) to believe it is because they are lacking in enough faith.

Thankfully, the Holy Spirit prompted John to include the incident of the paralytic at the Pool of Bethesda in his Gospel account. When Jesus encounters this man and asks him a simple question, "Do you want to get well?" the man does not even answer him. Instead, he tells Jesus all the reasons why he can't get well: it has already been thirty-eight years, no one will help him to get to the healing waters of the pool and so it is impossible for him to get there on time. We see no sign of the paralytic exercising any degree of faith. So, on the basis of our clearly defined principles of healing, obviously nothing can happen. But Jesus is not confined by our expectations or standards of judgment. Without rebuking or even pointing out the man's lack of faith, Jesus simply tells him to stand up and walk, once again shattering our assumptions of who he is or how he should act. To begin the journey of praying for the sick is to be confronted by mystery. As St. Augustine wrote, "if we understand God, then he isn't God." Who *is* this King of Glory?

Jesus Heals Sin

Jesus is teaching a large group crowded into a house. Four friends, determined that Jesus will see their paralytic friend, lower him through the roof of the home. This well-known episode shows the power of human compassion to bring people to Christ and to change the possibilities. All the synoptic Gospels note that it was the faith of the friends that Jesus saw, not necessarily the paralytic's. In the Gospels, often, but not always, there seems to be an atmosphere of faith needed to facilitate heavenly activity. Everyone present assumed that the man's need was physical healing, but Jesus focused on his greatest need: forgiveness of his sins. This both surprised and offended some of the onlookers. Ironically, the religious leaders did not realize the depth of truth that they declared with their charge that God alone can forgive sins. Jesus' response went to the heart of a great truth:

Why do you raise such questions in your hearts? Which is easier: to say to the paralytic, "Your sins are forgiven," or to say, "Stand up and take your mat and walk"?
(Mk 2:8-9)

Jesus declares that it is harder for sin to be forgiven than for the paralytic to walk. The power of sin is a universally destructive force that leads to death. Sin has held humanity captive since the Fall of Adam and Eve. It is manifested in individual sins, but is itself a dark force that has remained beyond our capacity to defeat. When we focus on individual sins we are minimizing the incredibly destructive force of the power of sin. In his response to a legalistic and small understanding of sin, Jesus was pointing to something much bigger. This episode directs us toward both the Cross and resurrection. First, Jesus granted forgiveness of sins which would be fully displayed at the Cross; then, by healing the paralytic, he displayed the future power of the resurrection.

... And Even Death

Jesus Delays

The raising of Lazarus is recorded in more detail than any other healing or miracle in the New Testament. This narrative must be observed at two levels in order to gain a right understanding. Lazarus is part of a family that is particularly close to Jesus. Theirs is a home where he can retreat to rest and recover. Yet, when told of Lazarus' serious illness, Jesus delays two days before setting out. When he arrives, Lazarus has been dead for four days, by which time, according to Jewish tradition, his spirit has left his body. Jesus allows Lazarus and his sisters to suffer. This may challenge our understanding of the compassionate One, but in delaying, Jesus is teaching that sickness and death are part of the brokenness of our fallen world. None of us, no matter how obedient and faith-filled we are, get a pass on this. Yes, Jesus heals. I have seen this too many times to ever doubt that. But we still must confront death and suffering that will never be eradicated from this life until he returns. Suffering is not caused by God to punish; rather, suffering is one way that we are conformed progressively into his image. That is why Paul wrote, "That I might know him and the fellowship of his sufferings."

When Jesus said publicly in front of Lazarus' tomb, "Thank you Father that you have heard me," we are reminded that Jesus only did what he saw the Father doing (Jn 5:19). Therefore, it is likely that for two days, instead of coming to Bethany, he was praying, waiting for the Father to guide him in perfect timing.

Living Between the Times

When Martha comes to Jesus, she says, "If you had been here my brother would not have died." Jesus responds,

> *I am the resurrection and the life. Those who believe in me, even though they die, will live, and everyone who lives and believes in me will never die. Do you believe this? She said to him, "Yes, Lord, I believe that you are the Messiah, the Son of God, the one coming into the world." (Jn 11:25-27)*

There is a lesson here in how we see Christ's interaction with us. We can have more faith for what he has done in the past ("If you had been here") and for what he will do in the future, than what he is doing right now. How often our churches focus on the great things that God did long ago, either in Bible times or in the traditions of our various denominations. Other churches focus on the future, looking ahead to the great revival that is bound to come soon. This is because it is so hard for us to live in the tension of "the already-and-not-yet" of the Gospel. This in-between time is filled with paradox and unanswered questions—mystery. Jesus brings the future into our present. Jesus is *already* the resurrection and the life. His resurrection power is for us to experience in the present. This is a great part of being "in Christ."

Anger and Sorrow

> *When Jesus saw her crying, and the Jews who had come with her crying, he was angry in his spirit and deeply moved. (Jn 11:33 CSB)*

John is bringing us closer to Jesus' final confrontation with death. As he comes near to it, anger against this final, terrible foe rises up.

Moments later, Jesus weeps. We will never see a clearer picture of Jesus in his full humanity than this episode at Bethany. He weeps over the death of his friend and the pain that it is causing others. He weeps because he is confronted by the pain of humanity in the face of weakness and death. When the Son of Man, the second Person of the Godhead weeps, God is weeping with the world. Full identification. Full participation.

> *Surely he has borne our griefs*
> *And carried our sorrows (Is 53:4 ESV)*

Jesus enters deeply into the human condition. Jesus was grieving for what he was soon going to experience. He knew the pain his own death would cause his family, disciples and friends. Jesus Christ saves as the Son of God, and he feels as the Son of Man.

There are depths of meaning that reach beyond even the amazing event of a man who lay dead for four days being brought back to life. St. Augustine tells us that in saying that Lazarus is only sleeping, Jesus is foreshadowing what is to come for everyone, since all those who die in faith will be raised again and so they, too, are only sleeping. St. Athanasius wrote that the voice which called out, "Lazarus, come forth!" is the voice that spoke the world into creation, and the One that will call us from the tomb on the last day. At this tomb, mystery is revealed. Jesus is living in the already-and-not-yet of the Kingdom—Christ beyond time.

A few more thoughts on Lazarus

For me, perhaps the most profound lesson is that there can be no resurrection without first death. When following Jesus leads me at times on a path that is marked by failure, sadness, disappointment, and confusion, I must hold onto this truth. Jesus is allowing who I thought I was to die—Thomas Merton called this the false self—so that the one who is truly me, the one that the Triune God has held as the apple of his eye from the beginning of time, can rise up. This is resurrection power that comes from the reality of heaven and from bringing dead places back to life.

There can be no getting around it: Jesus allowed Lazarus to die, and in that death, his glory was revealed. Christ is always good; therefore, he works even in the bad things that are the outcome of both my sin and living in a fallen world. He uses everything for his final good in my life, both now and into eternity. This takes trust and is why I must never cease in my journey of learning to abide in him. The Lazarus story challenges me to neither avoid pain or loss, nor ignore or downplay it. Fellowship with Jesus means that I too will weep. I too will grieve at the injustice of suffering and death.

Bread and Mystery

The only miracle recorded in all four Gospels is the feeding of the five thousand. There are a number of Old Testament allusions found in this miracle. Since early days, the significance of the number of loaves—five—has been written about. Five is both the number of grace and the symbolic number associated with Moses who wrote the first five books of the Old Testament. By multiplying the five barley loaves, Jesus is transforming the Mosaic Law into something much bigger, greater, and more nourishing.[97] Jesus is the One who would come "like unto Moses" (Dt 18:15). Elisha multiplied twenty barley loaves so as to feed 100. Jesus now fed 5,000 with five barley loaves.

This miracle begins with Jesus' hearing about the execution of his cousin John. His response is very human; he goes out into the wilderness to pray. Yet even in his sorrow, when the people follow, he sets his very real feelings aside and, moved with compassion, feeds them. We see the prophetic connection with Israel in the wilderness receiving manna. Surely many in the crowd would have connected the two events.

---

97   Dr. M. d'Ambrosio, *Hidden Meaning of the Loaves and Fishes,* (Crossroads International https://www.crossroadsinitiative.com/ media/articles/hidden-meaning-of-the-loaves-fishes)

Overarching all of the Old Testament allusions is the centrally displayed truth that the abundance of God's grace is poured out upon his creation. There will always be enough and everyone receives their fill, with twelve baskets left over. In the Kingdom there is no exclusion. Christ's grace and mercy are without limit and shared without condition. The crowds that followed Jesus were predominantly from the uneducated, lower class. They were the "sinners" that the religious leaders avoided at all costs. Like the parable of the banquet, this meal is for anyone who will come (Mt 22). This miracle foreshadows the new covenant meal of God's people, the Lamb's Supper.

John wants us to see that this miracle not only points backward as confirmation that Jesus is the Coming One; it also points to the future. The day after the feeding miracle, Jesus addresses the masses, telling them that, because of what they have just witnessed, they must now recognize that he is the Bread of life that has come down from heaven. He then makes the radical statement that they must eat his flesh and drink his blood if they are to have life in him. Feeding the five thousand points directly to the Eucharist, what the early church called "the Great Mystery."

Isaiah presented the picture of an abundant feast as an image of God's restoration of abundant life.

> *On this mountain the Lord of hosts will make for all*
> *peoples a feast of rich food, a feast of well-aged wines,*
> *of rich food filled with marrow, of well-aged wines*
> *strained clear.*
> *And he will destroy on this mountain the shroud that is*
> *cast over all peoples, the covering that is spread over all*
> *nations; he will swallow up death forever.*

> *Then the Lord God will wipe away the tears from all faces,*
> *and the disgrace of his people he will take away from all*
> *the earth, for the Lord has spoken. (Is 25:6-8)*

In light of this prophecy, we should see the feeding miracle as carrying importance beyond the surface reading of 5,000 people receiving food. It is a prophetic act, pointing to the day when the Lord will invite *all* people to feast upon his eternal goodness. This miracle points to the victory won at the Cross. He will swallow up death forever for *all* people. The feeding is a sign and manifestation of that joyous victory.

Christ is In his Creation

Jesus Christ is fully human and at the same time fully God; he, therefore, is the link between earth and heaven. Every miracle reveals his true nature, his glory.

> *A great windstorm arose, and the waves beat into the boat,*
> *so that the boat was already being swamped. But he was*
> *in the stern, asleep on the cushion, and they woke him*
> *up and said to him, "Teacher, do you not care that we are*
> *perishing?" And waking up, he rebuked the wind and*
> *said to the sea, "Be silent! Be still!" Then the wind ceased,*
> *and there was a dead calm. he said to them, "Why are you*
> *afraid? Have you still no faith?" (Mk 4:37-40)*

Jesus radiates the glory of the Triune God. This episode is not a moment of power or authority; this is who Jesus is all the time. Jesus shows us a window into an eternal and unwavering reality: there is no place, no situation, no time where Christ is not present. He is *in* the elements of the storm. That is why he has control over them. Here is a picture of the movement of the entire cosmos. With all its wonder, mysteries, and vastness, the universe moves the way it does because not only does it express Christ, it *is* the movement of Christ. The creation is inseparable from the Creator. The disciples did not understand this; that is why they were afraid. They saw creation—in this case, the wind and the waves—as something outside of Christ. Until now they saw him as a marvelous teacher, healer, and deliverer. They were even beginning to see him as a savior, but now they were confronted with an almost infinitely bigger truth. Jesus is Lord over creation because he is in all parts of what he is always creating. Their fear revealed the limits of their understanding. This is why Jesus challenged them to not be afraid; instead, see the world through a new paradigm. "Don't look at the huge waves and raging wind. Look at me!" This was not Jesus trying to instill faith in them; it was Jesus showing them his true identity. More than a healer, he is the One who holds everything together in every time, in every place (Col 1:17).

A Wedding Feast

The Gospel of John has been called the most mystical, pointing to the eternal, cosmic reality of Christ. It is the most layered Gospel, rich in metaphor and allegory. John's Gospel contains only seven miracles or signs, much less than in any of the synoptic Gospels; however each contains details that reveal the divinity of Jesus and the centrality of his mission. It is noteworthy that John refers to them as signs, rather than miracles. Signs always point to something. John is telling us that each sign is pointing to Christ's final mission. This is never more true than in his first sign, turning water into wine at the wedding of Cana.

> *On the third day there was a wedding in Cana of Galilee, and the mother of Jesus was there ..."They have no wine."... Now standing there were six stone water jars for the Jewish rites of purification ... Jesus said, "Fill the jars with water." And they filled them up to the brim. he said to them, "Now draw some out, and take it to the person in charge of the banquet." ... "Everyone serves the good wine first and then the inferior wine after the guests have become drunk. But you have kept the good wine until now." Jesus did this, the first of his signs, in Cana of Galilee and revealed his glory, and his disciples believed in him. (Jn 2:1,3,7-8,10-12)*

Throughout Scripture, *the third day* carries great importance. Moses went up to Mount Sinai to receive the Law on the third day and encountered Christ as a theophany; Joshua (again, after encountering Christ; Joshua 1:1) and Israel prepared themselves to enter the Promised Land on the third day. These and many more examples all point to the central event in all of history, in fact, all of the universe: the three days of Christ's death, descent and resurrection. It is striking that the first sign, the event that begins the journey to the Cross, does not take place in the Temple or even a synagogue; rather, it is at a wedding feast. This speaks of the sacredness of all of life. This is a celebration, a time of great joy. Surely John is telling us that the Gospel is beautiful and brings joy; in fact in the words of Alvin Kimel, we are "destined for joy." Also, this wedding feast reminds us of the eternal joy that exists within the activity of the Trinity, and that we are invited into that "divine dance." Thirdly, this wedding points forward to the Lamb's Supper at the summing up of all things (Rev 19:6-9), and so, while it was an historical event, it also holds meaning beyond itself, serving as a prophetic type of a greater event.

In the Scriptures and throughout Semitic cultures, wine represented life. When Mary tells Jesus "they have no wine," it suggests that the old covenant was not able to bestow life upon anyone. The six stone pots were there to wash one's hands in order to be ritually pure, but miraculously, now they contain the best wine. This is at the heart of the water-to-wine gospel. It is full of meaning: from the Law of Moses to Christ, "full of grace and truth"; from the old covenant that washes to the new covenant that transforms.

St. Cyril, a church Father, has written:

"He set forth wine better than the first, for the letter kills, but the Spirit gives life. And the law has no perfection in good things, but the Divine instructions of Gospel teaching bring in fullest blessing. The ruler of the feast marvels at the wine: for every one, I suppose, of those ordained to the Divine Priesthood, and entrusted with the house of our Savior Christ, is astonished at his doctrine which is above the Law."[98]

---

98   St. Cyril, *Commentary on John Bk II*

This episode provides us with an interpretive key for reading the rest of John's Gospel. It teaches us to read the Scriptures in a new way, taking us from the literal meaning to the spiritual, allegorical meaning.

In this process is found a richness that carries us further into the mystery of Christ. This requires humility as we read and contemplate, coming as children (Mt 18:2-5), never relying on what we have understood before and believing that Christ has new mysteries to unveil. That is why St. Isaac wrote,

> "Never approach the words of the mysteries that are in the Scriptures without praying and asking for God's help. Say, 'Lord, grant me to feel the power that is in them.' Reckon prayer to be the key that opens the true meaning of the Scriptures."[99]

John completes this episode by telling us that Jesus manifested his glory. The revealed glory in this encounter is found in all the layers of meaning within that event. That is why pursuing the mystery of Christ in the Scriptures is vital if we are going to go forward in our journey toward his unsearchable riches.

---

99   Isaac the Syrian, *Ascetic Treatises*, cited by Olivier Clement, *Roots of Christian Mysticism*, p. 101

Mystery in the Message

> "The deepest theme of Jesus' preaching was his own mystery, the mystery of the Son in whom God is among us and keeps his word."[100]

Having looked at how the mystery of Christ is revealed through his actions, we now turn, albeit briefly, to Jesus' teaching. The greatest example of his teaching is found in the Sermon on the Mount. Throughout, it is counter-intuitive and often shocking, expressing the upside-down reality of the Kingdom of God. It confronts and challenges assumptions at both individual and societal levels. It surprises us, but it is fairly straightforward in its meaning. However, it is Jesus' parables that present us with mystery at the deepest level of his teaching.

The parables confront us with paradox, revealing Jesus as the One who has come, yet also the One who *will* come throughout human history until his final coming. Often, their enigmatic nature has led to making assumptions about their meaning that may lead us astray from Jesus' purposes. For example, when he is addressing immediate consequences to actions or attitudes, if we push Jesus' words off to meaning final judgment, we miss the central point of his words. One of many examples is the Olivet Discourse in Matthew 24. Jesus is giving a prophetic warning regarding the destruction of Jerusalem which indeed happened in 70 AD. By assuming that Jesus is talking about end times, we completely misunderstand

---

100 Joseph Ratzinger, *Jesus of Nazareth, Vol II*, (Ignatius Press, 2007), p.188

his meaning—a warning calling for the Jews to repent *right now*, or face dire consequences from the Romans. Whether we understand those consequences to be immediate or final, Jesus unveils life as it should be lived right now. The parables lead us to the mystery of God and his ever-present work in the world; they show us that God is not distant, he is the Father who both sees and acts. Jesus tells stories that reflect how God's light shines through in the midst of the ordinary, the everyday. It is their "everyday" quality that gives the listener every opportunity to connect with eternal truth; Jesus' parables reflect his unwavering inclusiveness. Perhaps more than anywhere in scripture, the parables invite us into more contemplative reading; it may be fruitful to approach each parable as a personal invitation from Jesus into his mysteries. In many of the parables we can all too easily assume that we understand the point or moral and move on, but in doing so we are like the tourist who takes a photo of something famous, and moves on to see the next site. The richness is found in the pondering. St. Jerome put it beautifully:

> "The Scripture's Gospel is shallow enough for babes
> to wade in and never drown and yet deep enough
> for scholars to swim in and never touch bottom."

The disciples recognized the mysterious quality to parables when they asked him, "Why do you speak to the people in parables?"

While Jesus' parables invite all, he knows that some will exclude themselves. Some listeners are too self-satisfied, self-righteous, or blinded by prejudice to hear what Jesus is saying. His parables require our collaboration;

we must enter the stories, recognizing ourselves and God in them. Jesus' response the disciples' question was to quote Isaiah,

'Hearing you will hear and shall not understand,
And seeing you will see and not perceive;
For the hearts of this people have grown dull.
Their ears are hard of hearing,
And their eyes they have closed,
Lest they should see with their eyes
and hear with their ears,
Lest they should understand with their hearts and turn,
So that I should heal them.' (Mt 13:14-15 NKJV)

Jesus is addressing a voluntary blindness and deafness. Some choose to continue in their hard-heartedness, which elsewhere Jesus calls out as wickedness. But even this passage presents the hope of restoration, that by changing their hearts they can be healed. Jesus quotes Isaiah to emphasize that the self-righteous do not *understand*. This word means so much more than comprehension or cognitive assent. The literal meaning is to stand under, that is, to be obedient to what Jesus is saying. True understanding always leads to a change of heart, thinking, or direction—*metanoia* (repentance).

Immediately, Jesus contrasted the hard of heart with the disciples: "But blessed are your eyes, for they see, and your ears, for they hear" (Mt 13:16). The parables are an open door and a gift for the innocent, for those who are receptive and prepared to hear and respond to Jesus' revealed light, and to let it change their direction and hearts.

Joseph Ratzinger (Pope Benedict XVI) observed that the Cross is the interpretive key for all of the parables. They speak in a hidden way that reveals something of the mystery of Christ, the Kingdom, and the Cross. Ratzinger points to the Parable of the Sower as an excellent example, where Jesus is both the seed that brings life to the soil that receives it, and to the truth that in order for that seed to bear fruit it must die.[101] Jesus' parables consistently address the issues of selfishness and ego (e.g. the unforgiving servant; the two sons; the tenant farmers; the rich man and Lazarus). Even parables which we think we *understand* are filled with enigma that is all too easy to pass over, unaware. Chris Green gives a striking example in the Prodigal Son:

> "The elder son, who never left home, admits at last
> that it has for him always been a far country. And
> in the end, he is a stranger from his father, who
> has neglected him for years, and from his younger
> brother, who is now too caught up in his own
> celebration to come out to greet him."[102]

The point is not to solve the enigma, but to let it carry us deeper into Jesus' message as mystery, be it the parable of the shrewd manager (Lu 16); the nature of the gulf between the rich man and Lazarus; or what Jesus meant by the outer darkness (e.g. Mt 8:12). Often, the longer we look, the greater the mystery.

----

101 Joseph Ratzinger, *Jesus of Nazareth, Vol II*, p.190
102 Chris E.W.Green, *All Things Beautiful*, (Baylor University Press, 2021), p.108

"The teachings of Jesus begin in story and end
in symbol—they begin in parable and end in us.
These are not Bible stories that we learn; these are
our stories."

Leonard Sweet

CHAPTER 8

The Glory of Christ

*For God, who said, "Let there be light in the darkness,"
has made this light shine in our hearts so we could know
the glory of God that is seen in the face of Jesus Christ.
2 Cor 4:6*

Glory (*doxa*) is a major theme in both Testaments. It refers to both the glory that is the reflection of who God is, and the glory that we give in praise and honor to him. Jesus told Martha that if she will believe, she will see his glory. John, after being on the Mount of Transfiguration, wrote about sixty years later, "We have seen His glory, the glory of the One and Only, who came from the Father, full of grace and truth." (Jn 1:14 NIV) What John saw marked him for the rest of his life. The Transfiguration is about the glory of God coming to earth. It is one of the most important, and mystical, events in the Gospel narrative. Read carefully and contemplatively, it will lead us into a greater revelation of Christ.

The church fathers insisted the Gospels were holy ground, to be approached as though on the threshold of a palace. They call us to an acute spiritual sensitivity. St. John Chrysostom, one of the foremost church fathers, admonishes us to "yield up our hearts to the Spirit."

> "I entreat you to follow us with much diligence, so
> as to enter into the very ocean of the things written,
> with Christ for our guide at this our entering in."[103]

Chrysostom goes on to say that we are to read "with a mystical silence." He compares this to a hushed audience in a theater waiting with great anticipation before the letters of the King are read. Nowhere is this more true than what we encounter in the Transfiguration of Jesus Christ. It is as if the curtain between the heavenly and earthly realm has momentarily lifted, making everything clearer and more *true*, and therefore, toward the reality of who we will be, and how we will live with him forever. At the Transfiguration we behold the life for which we were created—eternal and infinitely glorious.

> "We are glimpsing the timelessness of eternity
> breaking in on the present time. On that mountain,
> we are seeing 'through' the veil that separates
> Heaven and Earth and glimpsing the Kingdom of
> God in all its glorious indescribable essence—"bright
> shining as the sun," as the hymn has it."[104]

Jesus' baptism initiates his ministry; the Transfiguration inaugurates the next phase which will shortly lead to the Cross. It is so multi-layered in meaning and significance that one is challenged to know where to start or end. Certainly the Transfiguration underlines the reality of the Incarnation, the Trinity, and the breaking in of heaven into our earthly realm. It reveals Jesus as the only

---

103 John Chrysostom, *Homily One on the Gospel of St. Matthew*
104 J.D. Walt, (seedbed.com) np

Son of God who shares the Divine nature with the Father. St. Ephraim wrote:

> "He took them and led up the mountain and showed them how He was going to come on the Last Day in the glory of His divinity and in the body of His humanity."[105]

The Transfiguration leads us from the temporal to the eternal, from the earthly to the heavenly. It teaches us how to approach the Scriptures with spiritual, "water-to-wine" understanding.

> *And he was transfigured before them, and his face shone like the sun, and his clothes became dazzling white.*
> *(Mt 17:2)*

The Transfiguration

In some church traditions, the Transfiguration tends to be passed over somewhat briefly. Since it is filled with mystery, again we see the influence of the historical-critical method, leading us to limit our reading of these few verses at the literal level. However, as one Orthodox theologian has written,

> "The Transfiguration must be recognized as the greatest miracle of divine revelation. In the light of the Transfigured Christ, we can see the kingdom of heaven, the Trinitarian life of God, the mystery of

---

105 St Ephraim, *On the Transfiguration of the Lord* (https://liveandpray.org/blog/2020/8/19)

the church, and the mystery of our own salvation. We can see our invitation to a union with the mystical body of Christ, a union with his own divinity, with the source, the truth and the mystical principle of all life."[106]

The Transfiguration is recorded in all the Synoptic Gospels. Like his baptism, this is a central event in Jesus' life and ministry. In all three accounts, it takes place immediately after Peter's confession, "You are the Christ, the Son of the living God." This is followed by Jesus telling the disciples that he and they are about to go up to Jerusalem where he will suffer and die at the hands of the religious and political powers. He finishes this with a difficult saying, "There are some standing here who will not taste death until they see the Son of man coming in His kingdom." There have been various interpretations of this over the centuries, including that Jesus is speaking about the fall of Jerusalem in AD 70, or about the coming of the Holy Spirit at Pentecost. However, most of the early church believed that Jesus was referring to the Transfiguration, where the glorious reality of the Kingdom of Heaven would be revealed.

Just as when he healed Jairus' daughter and later entered into an agony of prayer in the Garden of Gethsemane, Jesus only took the three disciples closest to him: Peter, James and John. This time he took them up a high mountain. Traditionally, this is thought to be Mount Tabor, which is fairly close to Caesarea Philippi where

---

106 Andreas Andreopoulos, *This Is My Beloved Son*, (Paraclete Press, 2012) p.94

the previous chapter in Matthew took place. In the Old Testament, theophanies often took place where Christ came to men on mountains: Jesus came to Abraham on Mount Moriah; he came to Moses on Mount Sinai and Elijah on Mount Horeb. The mountain is the place of ascent toward God (Ps 121) and the place where we leave our commonplace life behind for a while. Throughout Scripture, mountains are the place of encounter. For Jesus in the New Testament, mountains were important: He went up a mountain to teach his greatest sermon; he often went up a mountain to pray in solitude; the risen Jesus directed his disciples to meet him on a mountain in Galilee for what would be their final earthly encounter with him.

In the early years of the church, Moses' journey up Mount Sinai was the metaphor used for our spiritual growth. However, after a few centuries, this shifted to the Mount of Transfiguration. On Sinai, Moses had asked God to see his face and was denied. On Tabor, he, Elijah and the three disciples saw the face of God. For the Jews, Sinai traditionally represented the Law. But, while it led to God, under the Law, the gap was still too great for humanity to see him. In a sense, Moses' ascent was incomplete. On Tabor, the quest to see God revealed was completed.

Matthew and Mark record that the Transfiguration took place six days after the episode at Caesarea Philippi; Luke writes that it was eight days later. So why the different timeline? Matthew and Mark are stressing that the Transfiguration is a foretaste of the "completion" of creation, the summing up of all things in Christ. Luke, on the other hand, is connecting the event to the resurrection. As Brian Zahnd has written,

"It's the spiritual-mystical reading of the Gospels as
inspired theopoetics that will lead us ever deeper
into the Paschal Mystery."[107]

The Mystery of Christ is not found on the surface of
things. It is right to start at the literal level, but then we
must look deeper. Origen, the deeply theological and
mystical church father, wrote:

"Do you wish to see the transfiguration of Jesus:
Behold with me the Jesus of the Gospels. There He is
beheld both 'according to the flesh' and at the same
time in His true divinity. He is beheld in the form of
God according to our capacity for knowledge."

Moses and Elijah

Much has been written about the meaning of Moses and
Elijah's appearance on the mountain. Most obviously,
Moses represents the Law and Elijah the Prophets. Moses
reminds us to look back at the faithfulness of God and
his promise throughout Israel's history. Elijah represents
the future promise of complete restoration. In Jesus' time
there was a great anticipation among the people that
Elijah would soon return to usher in the Messiah.

Brian Zahnd has given us a wonderfully poetic
description of what was happening as Jesus, Moses, and
Elijah spoke together on Mount Tabor:

---

107 Brian Zahnd, (https://brianzahnd.com/2021/10/six-or-eight-on-
reading-the-gospels)

"The Transfiguration is where Moses and Elijah find their great successor. The Transfiguration is where the Old Testament hands the project of redemption over to Jesus. The Transfiguration is where the old witness yields to the new witness. But with Christ, morning has broken, the new day has dawned, the sun of righteousness has risen with healing in its rays. Now the moon and the stars, Moses and Elijah, the Law and the Prophets are eclipsed by the full glory of God in Christ!"[108]

Jesus Christ has, according to his own words (Mt 5:17), fulfilled the Law and the Prophets. That is why the Father told the three frightened disciples to "Listen to *Him*," not to Moses and Elijah. For over a thousand years the Jews had been waiting for the fulfillment of the Mosaic promise of Deuteronomy 18:15: "The Lord your God will raise up for you a prophet like me from among you, from your fellow Israelites. You must listen to him." As modern readers in a twenty-first century context, it is easy for us to miss the incomparable prestige of Moses in Jesus' day. Among the Jewish people, Moses was held in reverence second only to God; given this, it is hard for us to imagine the force of the Father's words upon the three disciples. There will not be three tabernacles, as Peter proposed, because the Son of God is the one eternal tabernacle.

Above all else, we are to listen to what Jesus says. The Bible is not a flat text where every passage carries the same weight. The Old Testament is *not* on par with

---

108 Brian Zahnd, *Six or Eight?* (https://brianzahnd.com/tag/transfiguration/)

Jesus. As we have seen in an earlier chapter, Jesus is the interpretive key to understanding the Old Testament; he is also superior to it. We revere the Old Testament, but its authority is not equal to Jesus. That is why he says, "You have heard it said (Moses), but I say to you ..." I often wonder why there is so much more preaching from the Old Testament than the Gospels? Jesus never rejected the Law and the Prophets; he fulfilled them. The Transfiguration shows us the continuity of God's story and his plan for creation. The Transfiguration shouts to us the truth that the way to understand the Old Testament rightly is through relationship with Jesus.

Moses and Elijah also represent the living and the dead, and tell us that all are alive in Christ. Moses died and was buried; Elijah was taken into heaven without dying in order to appear again to announce the time of God's salvation in Christ. For both, death is no more. Life is eternal.

> *And as for the resurrection of the dead, have you not read what was said to you by God, 'I am the God of Abraham, the God of Isaac, and the God of Jacob'? He is God not of the dead, but of the living. (Mt 22:31-32)*

Luke records that they were speaking with Jesus about his *departure*; in the Greek, the word is *exodus* and this is the only place in all of the Gospels where it occurs. Luke is once again presenting more than one layer of meaning. He is talking about the journey that Jesus will soon be taking that will ultimately lead to his death. However, *exodus* speaks of God's great plan to bring ultimate freedom—eternal life—to his people which is the culmination of his great purpose. The Transfiguration demonstrates to us the continuity of God's story and plan for his creation. It is also a key marker in the narrative, moving Jesus toward his appointment in Jerusalem.

> "For He says listen to Him, rather than to Moses or the prophet who have been introduced, because it was now time to go forward and advance from the introduction to the fulfillment, from the prefiguration to the reality."[109]

The Light

> *There he was transfigured before them. His face shone like the sun, and his clothes became as white as the light. (Mt 17:2 NIV)*

The word translated as transfigured is actually *metamorphosis*, like a caterpillar becoming a butterfly. Perhaps John is hinting that on the mountain Jesus stepped into his own future, transformed into what he would fully be in eternity. The disciples are seeing Jesus for the first time as he really is. Maximus the Confessor understood the Transfiguration as a prism, refracting the dazzling light of the heavenly realm for those who come near and leading to a metamorphosis from natural to spiritual senses. Many years later, John would record His vision of heaven, Jesus' ultimate realm.

> *The city does not need the sun or the moon to shine on it, because God's glory illuminates it, and its lamp is the Lamb. (Rev 21:23)*

---

109 Apollinaris, *Ancient Christian Commentary*, p.56

After coming down from Mount Sinai, Moses' face shone for a time, but this was *reflected* light; Jesus *is* the light.

John did not record this event in his Gospel, most likely because by the time that he wrote it, what had taken place on Mount Tabor was common knowledge among the churches. However, for the rest of John's life, it left its mark upon all that he wrote. Without a lot of description or explanation, he declared: "God is light" (1:5), for this is how John encountered Jesus in his glory. Light became a constant theme for John; he wrote of it 21 times in his Gospel and letters.

> *In him was life, and that life was the light of all mankind. (Jn 1:4)*

> *Jesus is the true light who gives light to everyone. (Jn 1:9)*

> *When Jesus spoke again to the people, he said, "I am the light of the world. Whoever follows me will never walk in darkness, but will have the light of life. (Jn 8:12)*

> *I have come into the world as a light, so that no one who believes in me should stay in darkness. (Jn 12:46)*

What the three disciples saw was no ordinary light; it came from *within* Jesus and was now made visible externally. Because the Trinity is indivisible, this was the light of the Godhead. All three Synoptic writers try to find words to describe this light: "His face shone like the sun"; "dazzling white"; "whiter than any launderer could make them"; "his clothes were like lightning."

To more fully understand the impact of this dazzling light, we need to remember two sets of words describing

God: transcendence and immanence; essence and energies. In his transcendence God is wholly Other, completely beyond us, unfathomable. In his immanence the Triune God is with us, around us, and in us. His essence is that which is unknowable, completely beyond us. This is why God says in the Old Testament that no one can see him and live. Yet, as we saw in chapter two, there are many examples that seem to contradict this. The answer to this seeming contradiction is found in his energies, which are God in his activity and self-manifestation. Energies are what the Fathers meant by the activities of God that can be seen and experienced. The energies are what he *does*, that dimension of him that we can recognize.

St Basil wrote of God's essence and energies:

> "It is by His energies that we all may know our God; we do not assert that we can come near to the essence itself, for His energies descend to us, but His essence remains unapproachable."[110]

The light that the Gospel writers described was not an allegory, nor an abstract experience. The light was real; it was tangible. What the disciples saw and experienced were the energies of the Triune God penetrating the universe at that exact time and place. This divine light, beyond their ability to describe, was the outpouring of God's nature. The light was a manifestation of the energies which are the Trinity's existence outside of its transcendent essence.

---

110 St. Basil, (https://enlargingtheheart.wordpress.com/2016/01/02/basil-the-great-gods-energies-come-down-to-us-but-his-essence-remains-beyond-our-reach/)

The Cloud

"While he was still speaking, a bright cloud overshadowed them, and behold, a voice from the cloud said, "This is My beloved Son, with whom I am well pleased; listen to Him!" (Mt 17:5)

From the time of Moses God's presence was manifested in a cloud; the Old Testament referred to this as the *Shekinah*. God appeared as a pillar of cloud that both directed the Israelites and protected them from the Egyptians. The Law was given to Moses on Mount Sinai under the covering of a cloud. Later, at Solomon's dedication of the Temple, the Shekinah glory cloud appeared, so powerfully that no one could stand. Two hundred years later, the prophet Isaiah encountered the glory cloud and the angels filling the Temple with their cry of "Holy, holy, holy is the Lord of hosts!" Now on Mount Tabor, Jesus is the Temple and the Holy Spirit is manifested as the Cloud. Many of us have experienced being immersed in a cloud on a mountain or on the sea. The cloud disorients us and can be disconcerting. This certainly appears to be the disciples' experience. They had seen healings and miracles, but this is something quite different. It is as though they are leaving the certainties of time and space as they knew them and slipping into another, heavenly reality. Their response is not joy, but fear. However, this seems to be the most frequent response to encountering the glory of God. John, when he encounters the resurrected Jesus Christ sixty years later, falls on his face "as though dead." He is in good company: Ezekiel, Daniel, and Isaiah all had the same response to the unfiltered glory of Christ.

Origen saw the significance of the cloud in two ways.

"For a bright cloud of the Father, Son and Holy Spirit overshadows the genuine disciples of Jesus; or a cloud overshadows the Gospel and the law and the prophets, which is bright to him who is able to see the light of it in the Gospel, and the law, and the prophets."[111]

The Transfiguration and Baptism

The Synoptic Gospel authors are making the connection between the Transfiguration and Jesus' baptism. During both events the Father speaks audibly with almost identical words. There is a disturbance in the atmosphere. Mark records that at Jesus' baptism the heavens parted; on Tabor a cloud descended. Both episodes are Trinitarian events. There is a sense in which the disciples are immersed in the divine light and cloud. Historically baptism and the Transfiguration were connected; *baptismo* means to be immersed, just as the disciples were immersed in the divine Light and Cloud. At their heart, both events are about making God present *among* and *inside* us.

The Transfiguration and the Eucharist

There is richness to be found in considering the church as the transfigured body of Christ. Both are directly connected, for the transfiguration of the self includes becoming sacramentally linked to church. Like salvation, Christ's church *has* been transfigured into a living organism—His body;

---

111 Origen, *Homilies on the Gospel of St. Matthew, The Transfiguration*

it is also *being transfigured*, changed "from glory to glory"; and *will* be finally, fully, and eternally transfigured. This is the church's unshakeable destiny.

Jesus told the disciples that they would see the kingdom of God come in power (Mk 9:1). Jesus manifested both his presence and the kingdom on Tabor. He is present in his church; it is, after all, his Body. His presence is manifested sacramentally in the Eucharist, through what the early church called "the Great Mystery." It transcends time, looking back to the Crucifixion and ahead to his Second Coming. Thus we "remember" something that, chronologically, has not yet taken place, but in eternity, has already come. Through the bread and the wine of the Eucharist—the Body and Blood of Christ—we enter into sacramental time, participating in the presence of Christ and his kingdom in the here and now. On Mount Tabor the disciples were set apart (sanctified) and in that state, they participated in the Divine communion of the Trinity. This is what is both remembered and actualized at the communion table. In this great mystery, we the church are united with Christ, renewed by his life being taken into our lives, and being transfigured as we behold him (2 Cor 3:18).

The Trinity

As with the baptism of Jesus, the Transfiguration presents us with the activity of the Triune God. The curtain is lifted between heaven and earth, and the Trinity is revealed. The Holy Spirit descends upon them all, manifested as a bright light and cloud, awakening the spiritual senses of Peter, James and John. The Father speaks so that they may hear. Jews honored Moses and Elijah above all others, yet the Father does not tell the disciples to listen to them; there is One greater in their midst: his Son. He does not say "He has become My Son" but rather, he *is* my Son, expressing the unbreakable and eternal bond between them.

Here we see the interconnectedness of the Trinity. Jesus and the Holy Spirit both reveal the light of God's energies; they are inseparable, yet distinct. Just as Jesus continually throughout his life gives glory to the Father, now we see the Father and Holy Spirit glorifying Jesus. This demonstrates that each member of the Trinity gives himself to the others. This "given-ness" is the life source that resonates throughout all of the cosmos.

This trinitarian cloud that had manifested on a few occasions in Israel's past now is descending, enveloping the disciples in a merging of past and present, heaven and earth.

> "This is incomparable grace because the cloud was none other than the Holy Spirit himself. Beneath the cloud of the Holy Spirit, the disciples were together with the Father and the Son, enveloped in the infinite mystery of the Holy Trinity, and they were not dead; what extraordinary grace! They were not even at a distance from the Trinity but at the Trinity's very heart like no one had ever been."[112]

Sometime before this event, Jesus gave a prophetic hint of what was to happen. In Matthew chapter 13,

---

112 Philemon of Gaza, trans. Daniel Bourgnuet, *Philemon of Gaza Meditates on Matthew's Gospel* (The People's Seminary Press, 2024) p.196

Jesus explains the parable of the tares, saying, "Then the righteous will shine like the sun in the kingdom of their Father." In the Transfiguration, we are told that Jesus' face "shone like the sun" (Mt 17:2).

The transfiguration of the righteous would flow from the splendor of Jesus. Now, the disciples are brought into this divine communion. Being enveloped in the cloud of the Holy Spirit, they are included in the inexpressible love between the Father, Son and Holy Spirit. They are brought into the *perichoretic*, divine dance of the Trinity.[113] It is the disciples who are transfigured, in that their capacity to see Jesus as he truly has changed.

> "There was no change in Christ. What changed was that the Holy Spirit affected the way the three apostles saw their teacher. For the first time they could see his divinity, although he was always God, even when his divinity was hidden."[114]

This serves as a model for *deification*. As the Apostle Paul wrote, it is as we behold his glory, we are being transfigured, becoming more like Christ. It is not our effort, but our *beholding* that changes us.

---

113 ibid, p.198

114 Andreas Andreopoulos, *This Is My Beloved Son*, (Paraclete Press, 2012) p. 34

The Three Tabernacles and the Descent

*Then Peter answered and said to Jesus, "Lord, it is good
for us to be here; if You wish, let us make here three
tabernacles: one for You, one for Moses, and one for
Elijah." (Mt 17:4 NKJV)*

Peter's response reflects his desire to stay in this
wonderful experience of Divine union. Anyone who
has experienced a powerful encounter with Christ can
understand this desire. However, this experience is not
given to the disciples for its own sake. Rather, it is about
empowerment and revelation that would carry them
forward into the world. After this episode, Jesus knows
that his obedience to the Father's will would carry him
down the mountain and into his Passion and Crucifixion.
The same would be true for the disciples. "The visionary
experience of light points to the difficult path that leads
to the Cross."[115]

Jesus invites the three disciples up Mount Tabor not
just to see him in his true identity; he wants to strengthen
their faith for what was ahead, because as wonderful as
it was, the Transfiguration is a marker on the journey.
Having been in the middle of an historic renewal
movement thirty years ago, I witnessed the great pull to
try to keep in the middle of a very real experience, but
never go back down the mountain to reach all those in
need of Christ. Peter's proposal to build three tabernacles
is about more than building a memorial; it also provides
a reason to stay up the mountain. The Transfiguration is

---

115 ibid p. 104

a foretaste of the Kingdom of God, but for everyone, the road back down the mountain goes through the Cross.

The Power of Encounter

To a great extent, our experience is our life source; we are formed by it and it is a powerful force in how we see the world, God and ourselves. What took place on the mountain remained with the disciples for the rest of their lives. Years after Mount Tabor, Peter wrote,

> *[W]e had been eyewitnesses of his majesty. For he received honor and glory from God the Father when that voice was conveyed to him by the Majestic Glory, saying, "This is my Son, my Beloved, with whom I am well pleased." We ourselves heard this voice come from heaven, while we were with him on the holy mountain. (2 Pe 1:16-18)*

What the Father said at Jesus' baptism—"You are my beloved Son in whom I am well pleased"—he now wants the disciples to hear. In a very short time, Jesus would be tried and executed. For the rest of their lives the disciples would live in peril because of Jesus. The Transfiguration was a strengthening event for them, because they would need it. And so do we.

We were created for authentic relationship with the Triune God and that must include personal encounter with him. Without it, we stay in the place of theories and ideas about God. Without it, the Scriptures, instead of being a love letter, become a policy manual, telling us the right and wrong ways to do things. But with encounter, we enter into the dynamic, life-giving relationship for which we were created. No wonder the apostles spent the rest of their lives telling anyone who would listen about this marvelous Son of God. They had encountered him. They had seen him in his glorious and full reality.

It is striking that the Apostle Paul never speaks about his personal spiritual experiences, except when necessary; the Damascus Road being a prime example. Even when he needs to tell the Corinthian church about his "visions and revelations of the Lord" (2 Cor 12:1) he uses few words and attempts to distance himself in the telling:

I know a person in Christ who fourteen years ago was caught up to the third heaven. (2 Cor 12:2)

His goal and purpose was always to bring glory to Jesus Christ, not draw attention to his experience of Christ. With Paul's example in mind, I will attempt to recount some of my own experiences to illustrate the importance and power of encounter.

My Personal Journey

In 1977 as a young believer, I attended a retreat weekend for young adults. After one of the sessions, a few of us stayed behind to sing and pray among ourselves. Suddenly, I felt electricity jolt through me and then I was surrounded by a bright light. This went on for some time. I had no grid for what was happening, yet I was aware of the love of God pouring over me. Perhaps more importantly, as the weeks and months followed, I lived with a greater assurance of Jesus' love and presence. Several years later, while attending a large conference, the holy presence of God settled so powerfully that I lay on my face for a long time. After a while, I realized that everyone was in the same position. (The holy presence of the Lord was so strong, I cannot imagine that anyone would have remained standing.) Suddenly, I saw a picture or vision of a most beautiful garden. Without going into more detail, the Lord used this to awaken me to his calling in my life, which meant a radical re-direction.

Nearly ten years later, while I was praying for a friend, (again, suddenly and unexpectedly) the power of God hit me so hard that I could not stand or even move for hours. I cannot describe the wonder of this as I felt waves of his love pulse over and through me. It was power and light all at once. I had no way of knowing that through this encounter, the Lord was opening a door of intimacy and his abiding presence whereby he has met with me again and again throughout the years.

Like all lives, my journey has not been without challenges and dry seasons, but, punctuated by my history of "Mount Tabor" experiences with him, it has been undergirded by the strength of encounters with Christ. As Henri Nouwen has written,

> "Jesus wants us to see his glory, so that we can cling to that experience ... When we are attentive to the light within us and around us, we will gradually see more and more of that light and even become a light for others. We have to trust that the transfiguration experience is closer to us than we might think."[116]

---

116 Henry Nouwen, cited by Silas Henderson, (https://aleteia. org/2017/08/05/the-transfiguration-and-the-mystical-moment/)

The Heart of the Matter

The Transfiguration was a literal event; it was the fulfillment of all previous theophanies and manifestations of God throughout the Old Testament. In one sense, it summed up all that went before.

In looking at the Transfiguration, we have considered many factors to help us gain a better understanding of its significance as a high-water point in the Gospel account, including its setting and context; the meaning behind the appearance of Moses and Elijah; the Trinity, the glory cloud; and Jesus as the light. However if we were to stop here, we would be missing the forest for the trees. Any examination of the Transfiguration must revolve around two overarching issues: What does it tell us about who Jesus is, and what does it reveal about who, in eternity, we will be?

As we go beyond reading about, and instead enter *into* the Transfiguration, along with the three disciples we see Jesus Christ as he truly is—bigger than my personal Savior, more powerful than my Healer; greater than the One who is committed to hearing and responding to my prayers. He is all of these things of course, but as I take time to quiet my soul, something deep inside me begins to stir. Jesus is outside and beyond space and time, in fact he is outside any of my definitions and certainties. As I look at him in this event on the mountaintop, I begin to see a life that is completely Other, for Jesus is the Creator who entered what he created. Within him is contained the glory of the Trinity and the glory of heaven. The beauty and unfathomable vastness of the cosmos are alive within the transfigured One. His Divine Light, the energies of his being cannot be contained, shining with dazzling brightness upon everyone on the mountain.

All that happened here is a preparation for what was about to take place at the Cross, where Jesus would defeat sin, Satan and the power of death. In his self-emptying, his kenosis, I have see his brokenness and suffering. But when I look at the Cross through the Transfiguration, I see *who* was on the Cross: The Alpha and Omega who was, and is, and is to come beyond time. The Creator of the very wood that he chose to be nailed to— as well as everything else in the universe. Even at that moment, Christ was still creating. The One who holds *everything*—including those things that appall me—and embraces them in his purity and perfection. This is the One hanging on the Cross. This self-emptying love is the greatest revelation of his glory. And as we enter into the journey of beholding Jesus, we discover the paradox that mystics, contemplatives, and believers have articulated over the centuries. The closer we get to Christ, the more our hearts and spiritual vision are filled and transformed by him, and the more our longing for him increases.

Julian of Norwich was a fourteenth century contemplative whose revelations of Christ and the Cross have impacted believers for seven centuries. Like other contemplatives, Julian's life was marked by solitude, silence and an abiding hunger to better know Christ.

She described this phenomenon like this:

"I saw Him and still sought Him,
For we are now so blind and so unwise that we
never seek God until He of His goodness shows

Himself to us;
and when we see anything of Him by grace, then are
we moved by the same grace to try with great desire
to see Him more perfectly.
And thus I saw Him and I sought Him,
and I possessed Him and I lacked Him.
And this is, and should be, our ordinary behavior in
life."[117]

There is a wonderful promise in 2 Peter 1:4 telling us that our ultimate destiny is that we "may share in the divine nature." We will continue to be transformed until we become like God; not that we will ever share his essence, but we will share in his life, love, purity and glory. God created all of us in his own image (*Imago Dei*) and when Jesus was incarnated, he manifested that original perfect image.

On Mount Tabor, we see what we will become when that image is restored, a process called sanctification. Therefore, the Transfiguration not only reveals Jesus' divine glory; it shows us our potential and truest identity when he restores us to our original state—not depraved victims of the original Fall, but the beautiful and good creatures that he declared us to be. And this transformation, this metamorphosis, does not stop with you and me. The entire cosmos will be transfigured, with everything in it displaying the glory of Christ: his eternal, irresistible purpose for all he has created.

---

117 Julian of Norwich, *Revelations of Divine Love*, (Oxford University Press, 2015) p.53

At the Transfiguration, we see a preview of the resurrected Christ. When we look at him, we are looking at our glory-filled future, as resurrected humanity. Paul calls Jesus the second Adam because not only is he what God intended for the first Adam to be, Christ is the first of a whole new people. Both John and Paul express this clearly:

> *What we do know is this: when he is revealed, we will be like him, for we will see him as he is. (1 Jn 3:2)*

> *For if we have been united with him in the likeness of his death, we will certainly also be in the likeness of his resurrection. (Ro 6:5 CSB)*

The Apostle Paul, who suffered so much for the Gospel of Christ, was continually strengthened, and he in turn strengthened the churches, with the truth and power of our common future destiny.

> *Look, I will tell you a mystery! We will not all die, but we will all be changed, in a moment, in the twinkling of an eye, at the last trumpet. For the trumpet will sound, and the dead will be raised imperishable, and we will be changed. For this perishable body must put on imperishability, and this mortal body must put on immortality. When this perishable body puts on imperishability and this mortal body puts on immortality, then the saying that is written will be fulfilled:*
> *"Death has been swallowed up in victory.*
> *Where, O death, is your victory?*
> *Where, O death, is your sting?" (1 Cor 15:51-55)*

The more clearly I can see Christ on the mountain, the more clearly I can see my eternal, resurrected self.

Earlier I stated that our understanding of the Gospel can only be as big as our revelation of Christ. To meditate upon the Transfiguration, contemplating who he truly is and therefore who we truly are, is a sure gateway to a greater revelation. It is not just for Peter, James, and John that the curtain between heaven and earth, between time and eternity, opened. This climactic episode is an invitation to all of us: "Come up here."

Let us finish this chapter with the beautiful words of Father Kenneth Tanner:

> "And from this human and divine face, shining like the sun in full strength, everything in creation will in the end be transfigured by light, a consuming fire which reveals the true essence of all things, and redeems further still beyond all original goodness, heals from every participation in evil, elevates to participation in the divine nature."[118]

---

118 Kenneth Tanner, *Transfiguration and the Defeat of Death*, Clarion Journal for Religion, Peace, and Justice, Feb. 14, 2021

CHAPTER 9

The Final Mountain

I have lived much of my life near mountains: along the coastal range of British Columbia, and for a time, in the midst of the Rocky Mountains which rose up many thousands of feet all around us, seemingly straight up, delaying both sunrise and sunset. Now I live next to the Sandia Mountains of New Mexico, named for the watermelon color they display as the sun goes down. Mountains speak to my soul of majesty, beauty, and the sacredness of unspoiled silence. It seems that mountains were very important to Jesus, too; his connection to them runs throughout the Gospel account. During his temptation, he was led to a high mountain. A mountain in Galilee was the sight of his great sermon. On different occasions he went up mountains to pray to his Father. When Jesus wanted to get away from the crowds, it was to the mountains where he withdrew. As we have seen, the heavenly realm invaded the earthly on Mount Tabor. And now the Mount of Olives is introduced into the Gospel narrative. It will play a key role from this point onward.

The Mount of Olives

Jesus' final public sermon, recorded in Matthew 24 and 25, is known as the Olivet Discourse, named for where it was delivered. From this mountain Jesus looked over Jerusalem, knowing what was to happen to it within a generation, and wept. The Mount of Olives was the scene of great struggle. It was here in the Garden of Gethsemane that Jesus wrestled with dark powers as he began to experience what awaited him on the Cross. The Mount of Olives was also where he suffered betrayal, abandonment, and arrest. Luke recorded that about forty days later, Jesus ascended to heaven from this mountain. We can only wonder if Christ chose this place because of its prophetic significance.

In a vision, the prophet Ezekiel saw the glory of the Lord leave Jerusalem and ascend to the mountain east of the city—the Mount of Olives (Ezek 11:23). Several church fathers recognized that Ezekiel's vision pointed forward to the time when Christ would walk the earth. St. Jerome wrote that, "the glory of the Lord, which had departed from the city of Jerusalem, stood on the Mount of Olives as a sign of resurrection and light."[119] Eusebius points out that in his day, it was to Olivet that pilgrims came rather than Jerusalem. This was because the city had largely lain in ruins for centuries, with nothing left of the Temple. Zechariah prophesied that one day the Messiah would return and stand upon the Mount of Olives. When Jesus ascended to heaven in front of the disciples, this may have been a precursor to his ultimate return, which is why the angel said to the apostles,

---

119 St. Jerome, *Ancient Christian Commentary*, OT Vol 13, (InterVarsity Press, 2008) p.43

Men of Galilee, why do you stand looking up toward heaven? This Jesus, who has been taken up from you into heaven, will come in the same way as you saw him go into heaven.(Acts 1:11)

And now, at the beginning of what will be his final week, Jesus starts his descent down this same mountain, knowing full well what three distinct prophetic actions will set in motion.

The Triumphal Entry

Underlying tension has been steadily building in all four Gospel narratives. Jesus is heading toward the city that is the most dangerous for him, and his followers know it. Thomas even said to the others, "Let us go also, that we may die with him." (Jn 11:16) As Jesus begins to descend down Olivet, it is easy for us to imagine both his followers' fears and his determination, in spite of what he knows awaits. The time has come, and there will be no turning back. The time of concealment is over. Never again will Jesus say, "Tell no one."

Once again, Jesus is calling the disciples to an act of faith expressed in obedience. When he tells them to go into the town of Bethphage, on the eastern slope of the Mount of Olives, untie a colt and bring it to him, this challenges the disciples' trust. In first century Palestine, a donkey would have been so valuable it would often be shared by two or three families. Jesus is asking them to do something that seemed outrageous. I suspect that he is preparing them for the lifetime of extravagant faith and obedience that lay ahead. Perhaps to bolster their confidence, this is the first time that Jesus refers to himself as "the Lord," revealing his divine royalty. Jesus only did what he saw the Father doing (Jn 5:19); to ride in on this donkey was what the Father had revealed to Jesus. As Matthew points out in his Gospel, in their obedience, the disciples were fulfilling a 550 year old prophecy:

> *Tell the daughter of Zion,*
> *'Behold, your King is coming to you,*
> *Lowly, and sitting on a donkey,*
> *A colt, the foal of a donkey.' (Mt 21:5)*

This is a very intentional prophetic act that all Jews would have recognized from Zechariah 9:9. Jesus is acting out a type of living parable, establishing the nature of Christ's Kingdom. It is important to note that he was acting within the Scriptures, not simply expressing a self-initiated plan. The following verse in Zechariah's prophecy (10) declares that this King's dominion will stretch "from sea to sea" (which happens to be the motto of Canada, my country of birth). Jesus is bringing a Kingdom that will embrace the whole world. And he is a King who will always renounce violence and will accept suffering.

The Humble Entry

A Roman conqueror would come through the main gate of a city riding a white war stallion, yet Jesus comes down the mountain "lowly, and sitting on a donkey." *This* triumphal entry is thus a parody of the way the world expresses power. A donkey is the antithesis of a war horse, demonstrating once again that Jesus, in contrast with the world of empire, is non-violent. This ride down the mountain is a living parable that shouts a radically new reality.

The Jews were waiting, and had been for hundreds of years, for a warrior Messiah who would crush the oppressors and establish a righteous and just reign. This was their constant hope, and therefore the only way they could imagine Messiah coming. As I wrote in an earlier chapter, for much of the western church, the understanding of Christ's rule hasn't changed much. Since the fourth century when the church became a partner to empire, its history has too often been punctuated with moral compromise, coercion, force, and even violence. How many lives would have been spared, how many wars would have been avoided? If all of those who declared themselves to be Christians had refused to kill other Christians, neither World War One or Two could have ever begun. What if we had continued to follow the King who came down that mountain "lowly, and sitting on a donkey"?

The manner of Jesus' entrance into Jerusalem is important. There are two realities that must be held together. First, Jesus comes as a King. He is royalty sent by the Father ("Behold, your King is coming to you"). In every sense Jesus is fully the Messiah. At the same time, Jesus is the lowly King, unpretentious and humble. We must hold both of these truths together if we are to rightly understand his true identity and the nature of his mission.

> "They had a king who was gentle, for it was not God's pleasure to give an earthly kingdom to the powerful, but a heavenly kingdom to the gentle."
> (St. Bede, 8th C. monk)

We must not confuse Christ's coming in humility as weakness. He reveals the ultimate power of the Triune God by not resorting to violence or retribution on the Cross. The crucified Christ holds all power, but he uses that for the transformative power of good for his creation. The Zechariah prophecy that Matthew quotes continues:

> *I will cut off the chariot from Ephraim*
> *And the horse from Jerusalem;*
> *The battle bow shall be cut off.*
> *He shall speak peace to the nations (Zech 9:10 NKJV)*

Why Palm Branches?

Matthew and Mark report that the crowd cut branches and spread them on the road in front of Jesus. In John's account, they waved palm branches before him, singing Psalm 118. However, to the Psalm's "Blessed is the one who comes in the name of the Lord!" they added "the King of Israel!" This addition, along with the palm branches, is very illuminating. Palm trees were a symbol of Jewish nationalism.[120] (This was still the case one hundred years later when, after the successful Jewish revolt against Rome, coins were minted with the freedom symbol of palm branches.) Clearly, the crowd was welcoming Jesus as a national liberator. Surely he would triumph over the Roman oppressors and bring true justice according to their expectations (which of course they assumed were the right ones!). Just as clearly, Jesus' choice of a donkey was meant to counteract this assumption.

---

120 Raymond Brown, *The Gospel According to John, I-XII*, (Doubleday, 1966) p.461

The early Church saw great symbolic significance in the palm branches that were spread out on the road and waved in front of Jesus. Jerome saw Isaiah's prophecy, "prepare the way for the Lord" (Is 40:3), fulfilled as the branches were cut down and put along the way.

> "They cut branches from the fruit bearing trees with which the Mount of Olives was planted, and spread them in the way, so as to *make the crooked ways straight, and the rough ways smooth*, that Christ the conqueror of sin might walk straightly and safely into the hearts of the faithful."[121]

While it is good to avoid the mistake of seeing allegory in every detail of each verse, there is a richness waiting for all who will look more deeply into the Scriptures. Other church fathers saw a profound truth in the waving of the palm branches: they celebrated the Lord's victory over death. We see here the principle that the meaning of a Scripture is not limited to what the initial hearers would have understood. Romanus Melodus, an early composer of hymns wrote,

> "O Savior, all came with palms on the occasion of Thy arrival, crying out, 'Hosanna' to Thee …
> As we wave the branches of our spirit and cry out
> Incline Thy ear, O God of the universe, and hear our prayers, and snatch us from the bonds of death"[122]

---

121 St. Jerome, *Ancient Christian Commentary*, Mark, NT Vol II, p.148
122 ibid, John NT Vol IVb, p.52

Similarly, St. Augustine wrote,

> "The branches of palms are psalms of praise for the victory that our Lord was about to obtain by His death over death and His triumph over the devil, the prince of death, by the trophy of the cross."[123]

From "Hosanna" to "Crucify Him"

We may wonder how in only five days the crowd could go from such jubilation to attack. It is important to note that as Jesus was descending from Olivet, he was being followed by a crowd of Jerusalem outsiders. These were largely Galileans who were joining tens of thousands of other Jews on their way to celebrate the Passover. Like crowds in our day coming to a sporting event, naturally as they got closer to Jerusalem, the crowds grew. And, as the Gospel narratives tell us repeatedly, where Jesus went, crowds followed. These were Jesus' own people, the ones he had grown up with and had ministered to over the past three years. The crowds in Jerusalem were of a very different makeup, especially as the Passover festival swelled its population from about 30,000 to 180,000.

All four Gospels record that the crowds shouted out: "Blessed is He who comes in the name of the Lord!" This comes from the last of the six Hallel Psalms, a term meaning "praise." By Jesus' day, they were sung on joyous occasions, especially at the three major festivals. They describe a jubilant pilgrimage into the Temple. Matthew adds to this blessing, "Hosanna to the Son of

---

123 ibid, p.52

David"; Mark records, "Blessed is the kingdom of our father David." Clearly the crowd is welcoming Jesus as the Messiah, and as such, is engaged in a prophetic action of which they were likely unaware.

> "'Hosanna' in Hebrew signifies the redemption of the house of David. They are calling upon the Son of David. They are celebrating the inheritance of the eternal Kingdom."[124]

Here, as the crowd shouts Hosanna, it expresses the complex emotions of the Galilean pilgrims and of Jesus' disciples: joyful praise of God at Jesus' entrance blended with a hope that the Messianic Age had finally come.[125]

One early church father, Severus, believed that when the crowd cried out "Hosanna," they were proclaiming Christ's Second Coming. Of course they could not have known the weight of their words, once again demonstrating that when we choose to read Scripture at the spiritual level, hidden riches are unlocked.

Luke tells us that as the crowd with Jesus was about to enter the city, the religious leaders appealed to him: "Teacher, rebuke Your disciples!" There seems to be a serious, perhaps puzzling lesson for us here. When we encounter Christ's actions in ways that we are unfamiliar with, we have a choice. Our natural self, which Paul calls "the flesh," does not like to be confronted with people or situations that cut across our expectations. As the joyous, largely Galilean crowds shout out the Hallel, declaring

---

124 St. Hilary, *Ancient Christian Commentary NT Vol 1b*, p.127

125 Joseph Ratzinger, *Jesus of Nazareth, Vol II*, (Ignatius Press, 2011), p.7

that Jesus has come as the Son of David, the Pharisees'
position of power and security is being greatly threatened.
And so they resist, even refusing to see what is in front
of them. Jesus, always the lowly, humble One, does
not respond with anger toward the Pharisees. Instead
he speaks truth to them. First, all of creation is subject
to him so that even the rocks would cry out. He is the
eternal, infinite Creator, even if they cannot see it. Second,
their response does not anger Jesus, it breaks his heart,
bringing him to tears over Jerusalem. The third century
church father, Origen, applied this scene to his own day;
it is likely that it could also be applied to ours:

> "If Jesus had good reason to weep over Jerusalem,
> he will have much better reason to weep over the
> Church. It was built to be a house of prayer, but its
> shameful greed ... has made it a den of thieves."[126]

In this place of compassionate sorrow, Jesus tells
them that the very peace that they have been praying for
is now hidden from their eyes. Spiritual intransigence
has blinded their eyes, and the consequences will be cat-
astrophic beyond what they could imagine. Jesus sees
past, present, and future as one, but they will not hear.
No frustration, no anger, just sorrow. His sorrow will
increase throughout Holy Week.

---

126 Origen, *Commentary on Matthew*, cited by Olivier Clement in *The
Roots of Christian Mysticism*, **p.127**

Water-to-Wine

> *Above all, you must understand that no prophecy of Scripture came about by the prophet's own interpretation of things. For prophecy never had its origin in the human will, but prophets, though human, spoke from God as they were carried along by the Holy Spirit. (2 Pe 1:20-21 NIV)*

This episode presents us with the mystery of scriptural fulfillment. Beyond Jesus' demonstration of—in contrast with the worldly way of power—his humility and vulnerability lies another level of meaning. Christ is the One who lives throughout the pages of the Old Testament. Rather than think in a linear way, his triumphal entry blends past and present as one event. Isaiah, Zechariah and others declared what they saw in the future, but mysteriously; for Christ, who exists outside of time, this was already happening. As we see this, Old Testament details take on greater prophetic significance.

At the end of his life, Jacob gathers his sons to pray a blessing over each one. Jesus is from the tribe of Judah and so, through him, receives this prophetic blessing:

> *Binding his foal to the vine*
> *and his donkey's colt to the choice vine,*
> *he washes his garments in wine (Gen 49:11)*

As Justin Martyr points out, when Jesus had the donkey untied, he set in motion what would ultimately lead to the wine of eternal life for all. A seemingly insignificant detail uttered by an ancient patriarch is now seen in a very different light.

Jesus' choice of a donkey reveals a deeper mystery. Donkeys are mentioned more than any other animal in the Scriptures. Famously, Baalam's donkey refused to let him declare a curse over the Israelites. The Gentiles would not curse God's people. When God confronted Job he said,

Who gives the wild donkey its freedom?
Who untied its ropes?
I have placed it in the wilderness;
Its home is the wasteland. (Job 39:5-6 NLT)

The donkey is a beast of burden; to Job, it has obviously *not* been freed.[127] Therefore, it seems that God is speaking of a future event. Many church fathers saw the donkey as a type of the Gentiles. Here it is characterized as *wild*, living in a wasteland. Paul describes the wild Gentiles in Romans 11:17 "And you Gentiles, who were branches from a wild olive tree, have been grafted in."(NLT) When Jesus instructed that the donkey and its colt be untied, he was expressing an eternal and mysterious truth. Although he traveled all over Galilee and Judea, this is the only account of Jesus' riding on a donkey. A clear, intentional prophetic action.

---

127 Larry Shephard, *The Mystery of the Donkeys* (https://parablepower. com/Blog/the-palm-sunday-mysteries-the-mystery-of-the-donkeys, 2021)

Cleansing the Temple

Jesus entered the temple courts and drove out all who were buying and selling there. He overturned the tables of the money changers and the benches of those selling doves. (Mt 21:12 NIV)

According to Matthew's account, Jesus went directly from his entrance into Jerusalem to the Temple—two decisive prophetic actions in succession. They belong together, for each gives greater meaning to the other, revealing a Messiah whose mission not only surprised, but challenged, both the people's expectations and those of the ruling systems.

The first thing to see in this Temple episode is just how remarkably confrontational it was. From this point, there is no turning back. Jesus is directly challenging a socio-religious system that had zero tolerance for any demonstration or criticism of the way the Temple system was working. Yet why did the Temple guards not arrest Jesus? He is attacking the existing practice, but he is not violating the Law; in fact, Jesus was implementing the Law in a correct way.[128] This, of course, extends to any critique of its guardians: the priests, scribes or anyone in a position of religious authority. This episode is central to the rest of the Gospel; it is the impetus that will set the events of the Passion week in motion.

Why does Jesus begin with driving out those who bought and sold livestock and those engaged in currency exchange? Pilgrims came from far away, even beyond

---

128 Joseph Ratzinger, *Jesus of Nazareth Vol 3*, (Ignatius Press, 2011) p.12

Israel, to sacrifice animals. This activity was at its greatest height during Passover week. It was impractical for those who had traveled any distance to bring a lamb or goat with them; therefore they were compelled to purchase an animal at the Temple grounds. These animals were sold by Temple merchants at a significant profit. Also, the Roman currency that all travelers would be carrying, had to be converted into the acceptable Temple currency in order to pay the Temple tax or to make offerings. Again, this exchange was made at a large profit for the money changers. In our day, it is often taught that Jesus was condemning the practice of doing business in the Temple court, but that is likely not accurate. What he was coming against was systemic usury, taking advantage of the pilgrims, who as people living under Roman oppression, would usually come from the poor working class.

Defending the Poor

As always throughout his life and ministry, Jesus sides with the poor and is indignant wherever he sees injustice. He is so provoked that, as John tells us, "making a whip of cords, he drove all of them out of the temple, with the sheep and the cattle. He also poured out the coins of the money changers and overturned their tables." (Jn 2:15) In the Synoptic accounts, Jesus quotes Jeremiah 7:11: "You have made it a den of robbers." He attacks a system that treats the poor unfairly, even if it is centered in the Temple. The religious leaders thought that they were protected by God because they scrupulously held to the Temple tradition, but Jesus is demonstrating to them that God does not protect injustice that hides behind tradition and good appearances. Just as in his entry into Jerusalem, Jesus is directed by, and fulfilling, Scripture, not his own agenda. Notice that in all four gospel accounts, nowhere is it stated that Jesus is angry. He is obedient.

When confronted by the religious leaders regarding his authority to disrupt the sacrifice-market system, he replies: "Destroy this temple and in three days I will raise it up." As religious systems so often do, they chose to take Jesus' words literally, and later use them against him. They have missed the meaning of his words. It is not Jesus who destroys the Temple, but those who have abused it for their own gain. The sacrificial system stood at the heart of Israel's relationship with the Temple. By stopping it, even for a short while, Jesus is powerfully demonstrating that the Temple was under God's judgment—and prophetically pointing to the time, one generation away, when the sacrificial system would end forever. There is an irony present here; it is the Jewish leaders' rejection and crucifixion of Jesus that brought about the end of the Temple system. Beneath Jesus' words and actions lies a deeper meaning: the for-all-time sacrifice of Jesus on the Cross. The writer of the letter to the Hebrews emphasizes this repeatedly, for example:

> *And every priest stands day after day at his service, offering again and again the same sacrifices that can never take away sins. But when Christ had offered for all time a single sacrifice for sins, "he sat down at the right hand of God." (Heb 10:11-12)*

Christ is the new temple; the Jerusalem Temple was a time-and-space bound shadow of the true and eternal temple. But in this new temple, as Jesus told the Samaritan woman at the well, there will be true worshipers who worship in spirit and in truth (Jn 4:23). However, the religious leaders' adherence to tradition and its assumptions blinded them to see the mystery of the One who stood before them.

Just a few days later Jesus was with his disciples at the Temple, being confronted by these same religious leaders. He then turned to the disciples, in the hearing of all the people, and gave them a dire warning:

> *Beware of these teachers of religious law! For they like to parade around in flowing robes and love to receive respectful greetings as they walk in the marketplaces. And how they love the seats of honor in the synagogues and the head table at banquets. Yet they shamelessly cheat widows out of their property and then pretend to be pious by making long prayers in public. Because of this, they will be severely punished. (Lu 20:26-27 NLT)*

This is the context for what happens next. (The chapter break, which was not in the original, can cause us to miss this.)

> *While Jesus was in the Temple, he watched the rich people dropping their gifts in the collection box. Then a poor widow came by and dropped in two small coins. "I tell you the truth," Jesus said, "this poor widow has given more than all the rest of them. For they have given a tiny part of their surplus, but she, poor as she is, has given everything she has." (Lu 21:1-4 NLT)*

The more common application of this passage is to encourage us to give in faith even when our finances are very tight. However, in context, I believe that Jesus is not just praising the widow for giving her last two coins; rather, he is giving an indictment against this same religious Temple system that puts pressure on poor believers.

Making Room for the Outsiders

The Temple marketplace activity that Jesus so dramatically disrupted took place in the outer court, known as the Court of the Gentiles, because this was the one area where Gentiles were permitted. It was a large place where non-Jews could learn more about the God of Israel. They were not allowed into the more inner courts, nearer to God's presence. But they were allowed a more distant access where they could learn the Scriptures and learn about worship. They were strictly forbidden from entering any of the inner courts; signs were posted in Greek and Latin, warning that the penalty for trespassing was death. Yet seen positively, the Court of the Gentiles was an expression of at least limited grace, for here they could find out about God. This court had gradually been taken over by the Temple marketers.

When Jesus challenges the Temple leaders with, "My house shall be called a house of prayer," he is quoting Isaiah 56:7 "for my house shall be called a house of prayer for all peoples." This would almost certainly have been universally recognized. The Temple was supposed to be a sign of the inclusive love of God for all people. Instead, it had come to stand for the exclusive national identity and rights of the Jewish people. For the two thousand year history of the Church, there has always been this same pull toward exclusivism. However, Jesus demonstrated and taught a gospel that is always inclusive.

Matthew records something unique to his Gospel narrative.

> *The blind and the lame came to him in the temple, and he cured them. But when the chief priests and the scribes saw the amazing things that he did and heard the children crying out in the temple and saying, "Hosanna to the Son of David," they became angry. (Mt 21:14-15)*

There was a traditional saying, going back to when King David conquered Jerusalem: "The blind and the lame will never come into the house." Now here in the House, instead of rejecting them, Jesus welcomes and heals the blind and the lame. Matthew expects his Jewish audience to make this connection; that is why he repeats, "Hosanna to the Son of David," in sharp contrast to the offended chief priests. Here we are clearly presented with the contrast between those who live by the letter of the Law, and those who have eyes to see and hearts soft enough to encounter grace in their midst.

> "This is the true cleansing of the Temple. Jesus does not come as a destroyer. He does not come bearing the sword of the revolutionary. He comes with the gift of healing."[129]

---

129 Joseph Ratzinger, *Jesus of Nazareth, Vol II*, p.23

There is a water-to-wine reading available to us in this episode that invites us to examine our hearts. As Philemon of Gaza, a sixth century monk, has pointed out,

"To our great shame, there are merchants present, buying and selling within the precincts of our inner temple, making this text in the gospel very up to date and challenging. Who are these buyers and sellers? Might it not be ourselves because of the way we behave with God?. The temple is a house of prayer, but our prayers are often sullied by a spirit of commerce. Often we engage in trading with God.... We sell our works to God so that he will provide benefits in exchange."[130]

We so easily see our life in God transactionally. However, he is not a master to be negotiated with; he is our Father and we come as dependent and grateful children.

The Fig Tree Withers

Both Matthew and Mark present a third prophetic action, and like the preceding ones, it reveals more of the mystery of Christ beyond what is happening in the immediate. After the Temple cleansing, Jesus and his disciples go back up the Mount of Olives and spend the night in Bethany, presumably at the home of his dear friends, Mary, Martha and Lazarus. The following morning he again goes down the mountain and into Jerusalem.

---

130 Philemon of Gaza, trans. Daniel Bourgnuet, *Philemon of Gaza Meditates on Matthew's Gospel* (The People's Seminary Press, 2024), p.245

In the morning, when he returned to the city, he was hungry. And seeing a fig tree by the side of the road, he went to it and found nothing at all on it but leaves. Then he said to it, "May no fruit ever come from you again!" And the fig tree withered at once. When the disciples saw it, they were amazed, saying, "How did the fig tree wither at once?" (Mt 21:18-19)

While at first this incident may puzzle us, it expresses deep truth about the spiritual state of Israel and provides both warning and guidance for our day. The fig tree is one of the classic symbols of Israel through the Old Testament. We are reminded of the Fall in Genesis 3 where Adam and Eve, aware of their nakedness, tried to cover themselves with fig leaves. At the fig tree, Jesus encounters this sign of man's shame and disobedience that seeks to hide from God behind proper appearances.

In the Old Testament the fig tree often symbolizes the health of the nation both spiritually and physically, including its peace (Mic 4:4); prosperity (Joel 2:22); and the faithfulness of God's people (Zech 3:10). Hosea 9:10 says,

When I found Israel, it was like finding grapes in the desert; when I saw your ancestors, it was like seeing the early fruit on the fig tree.(NIV)

Conversely, Scripture also points to the fig tree to indicate judgment against the nation.

The vine withers; the fig tree droops. (Joel 1:12)

Do the vine, the fig tree, the pomegranate, and the olive tree still yield nothing? (Hag 2:19)

It is as though the fig tree was a barometer, measuring the health of Israel, exiled as punishment and flourishing in times of restoration.[131]

Knowing this, Jesus' meaning is fairly clear: He is predicting coming judgment upon Jerusalem.

There is no first-ripe fig for which I hunger.
The faithful have disappeared from the land, and there is
no one left who is upright. (Mic 7:1-2)

Like the fig tree, the days were coming when the city would be sacked by the Romans and left fruitless and withered. Judgment is coming to the Temple, the city, and the nation.

Cursing the fig tree is not a momentary act of irritation on Jesus' part; like his lament of Jerusalem that would follow closely after this, Jesus speaks with deep sorrow. Also, in this episode, Jesus is expressing care for the disciples. He knows that in a few days their faith would suffer its greatest test. It is vital that they understand that, just like his command over the fig tree, he is completely in control of the events that were about to unfold. John Chrysostom wrote:

"Do you see that He did all this for their sake, so that they might neither be afraid nor tremble with fear from the plots formed against them? On their

---

131 https://www.oneforisrael.org/bible-based-teaching-from-israel/figs-in-the-bible

account, he repeats this, in order to strengthen them in their devotion to prayer and faith."[132]

Speak to What Mountain?

Jesus' response to the disciples' amazement must have greatly challenged them:

Jesus answered them, "Truly I tell you, if you have faith and do not doubt, not only will you do what has been done to the fig tree, but even if you say to this mountain, 'Be lifted up and thrown into the sea,' it will be done. Whatever you ask for in prayer with faith, you will receive." (Mt 21:21-22)

This passage is often quoted as an example of what great faith can do. Clearly the Gospels consistently (although not exclusively—see Jn 5:6-8) link faith and miracles. However, this does not really fit with the context of what is going on with the fig tree. Perhaps we can see the meaning in Jesus' words more clearly by noting that he said, "If you say to *this* mountain." As he says these words, behind him stands the Temple Mount. Surely this was another warning about the judgment that was coming to the Temple and all it represented. Jesus' crucifixion and resurrection would begin a new age. God's presence would no longer be found at the Temple; now it would reside in the living temple of his Bride, the Church. It would be through the preaching and ministry of these same disciples that this living temple would

---

132 John Chrysostom, *Commentary on Matthew,* (The Church's Bible, Wm. B. Eerdmans Publishing Co. 2018) p.409

grow and the old Temple would, figuratively, be thrown into the sea.

Every "you" in this passage is plural. The promise of effective prayer is made to the praying community. As we collectively believe and do not doubt, as together we speak words of great faith, as we come together to "ask, seek, and knock," we will see God move on our behalf. Corporate prayer should find an important place in our life together. There is also a warning here. The Jewish leaders felt secure in their Temple practices; they were confident and comfortable with the status quo. But through the three prophetic actions we see that Jesus is exposing their fruitlessness. The great Anglican writer, pastor and evangelist Michael Green did not mince words:

"If there is no fruit (in prayerfulness, in evangelism, in love and ministry to the community), God will judge such churches and they will die."[133]

As Jesus came down from the mountain, the stage was set for a final tumultuous and climactic week that would change the destiny of the world. He came in humility and peace, but clearly he came as a King. The old order was coming to an end, but not without struggle and conflict. An entirely new reality had come, what E. Stanley Jones referred to as "the irresistible Kingdom."

* * *

---

133 Michael Green, *The Message of Matthew*, (IVP Academic, 2000) p.223

For several winters, every Monday night I went skiing with my oldest son. We lived close to a terrific mountain where, in less than an hour, we could look over the city. We pushed each other hard; I didn't want any son of mine beating me to the bottom, and he didn't want any old man beating him. One night we turned off the lit run and looked down at what seemed to us to be a sheer precipice. I remember our skis pointing into space as we decided if we had the courage to do this, knowing that once we committed, there could be no turning back. We pushed ourselves out and began what is still the single most memorable, exciting, and scary run of our lives. And, more than twenty years later, sometimes we reminisce about that run in the darkness. We both agree that our skiing changed for the better that night, carrying us to a new level.

While writing this chapter, my mind has gone back to that night a number of times. I imagine Jesus' friends and followers starting down their mountain, also knowing that, in this act, something would be set in motion that would be irreversible. We have looked at how his riding in on a donkey starkly contrasted with the entrance of a Roman victor. But there is something deeper going on. Like any work of art, creation reflects the heart of the Creator. There is a movement to creation, to the entire cosmos; it always goes in the direction and flow of mercy, forgiveness, humility, and unwavering compassionate love. As Jesus came down the mountain and into the Holy City, he was opening a door for the Jews, and ultimately all humanity, to enter into that Divine rhythm, to turn from resisting that flow to gratefully embracing it. This, after all, is what repentance—metanoia—means: to turn around, to change our way of thinking.

Jesus' Triumphant-Humble Entry challenged the religious system of his day, just as it should challenge our twenty-first century churches. More than at any time in America's history, a great swath of the evangelical church is trying to gain power and influence through the lever of politics. As we have seen, the Jewish leaders sought this with Herod and Pilate, just as the church did from the fourth century onward. So what we are seeing is nothing new; but it is distressing. Perhaps, like Jesus, it will bring us to weep over our cities.

In a recent text exchange with Bradley Jersak, he wrote the following:

> "It's as if the church somehow lost the irony of
> the kingdom metaphor (an upside-down reign
> of humble love and faithful martyr witness that
> overcomes through the blood of the Lamb and word
> of their testimony) and opted to pursue the route of
> a literal worldly empire ... Gratefully, the tradition
> from the time of Israel's first kings has always
> included a prophetic minority report willing to call
> [out the system], at the risk of their jobs and even
> their lives."[134]

Too often, leaders tell us that privilege and power are our right. "We are children of the King!" But who is this King of Glory (Ps 24:10)? We were expecting the One who would defeat our enemies and by his strength bring righ-

---

134 Brad Jersak text exchange, December 13, 2023

teousness to the land. Have our expectations blinded us to a King on a donkey? Jesus' entry exposes us to the universal temptation that he defeated at the outset of his ministry: the deepest longing for power, influence and authentication. Satan's temptation has not changed: "All this I will give you." (Mt 4:9) But our King told us, "Learn from Me, for I am humble and lowly." Collectively, as his Body and Bride, we either fully embrace this final reality or we compromise, and as Bradley wrote, we lose the irony of the upside-down Kingdom.

When I look at Christian nationalism and those of the evangelical church that trumpet it, too easily I can see *them* and miss what Jesus is saying to *me*. How easy it is for me to seek influence in my world. All too often I seek to subtly position myself to be thought well of, to impress, for my opinions to be respected and agreed with. But I am following the One who faced criticism, slander, mocking, and intentional misunderstanding. When my wounded pride wants to respond against the current of forgiveness, humility, gentleness and love, my lowly and humble King reminds me once again to lose my life in order to find true life.

A new kind of King brings a new way of worship, and that is why there is a certain inevitability to Jesus continuing from the streets of Jerusalem to the Temple. It was the center of Jewish society, and even more, the place where heaven and earth intersected with the presence of God. In a few days, Jesus would describe to his closest friends its total destruction, fulfilled within a generation. Like the Triumphal Entry, this meaning of Jesus' actions goes beyond clearing out animals and overturning money tables. He is challenging the Temple worship to be renewed, with anything that gets in the way of "spirit and truth" worship to be removed. The Temple, and our churches, are meant to be sacred space. What honors the sacred, pure and holy is that which we are to hold onto. We are reminded of the sixth Beatitude: Blessed are the pure in heart, for they shall see God.

As noted, Jesus challenged the priests with Isaiah 56:7, "For my house will be called a house of prayer for all nations." Today, Jesus challenges our churches to be culturally, racially, socially inclusive. Martin Luther King famously called Sunday morning at 11:00 "the most segregated hour in America." In the Kingdom of God "every tribe, tongue and nation" shall worship before his throne (Rev 7:9). Once again, I am challenged by Jesus' words. "All nations" calls me to an inclusive life, one that I choose to live beyond my boundaries of comfort and convenience, allowing God's totally *unbounded* love, acceptance, and care to re-form me.

In these three three distinct prophetic actions, I am challenged to not simply project their lessons to others. Jesus comes to *me* quietly and gently. Will I take time in the midst of the "crowds"—the busyness, those things clamoring for my attention, the incessantly invasive voices of social media and the news—to watch and listen for his still small voice? Will I clear out the clutter of my court, making room for both others and real worship? Will I settle for the camouflage, the leaves that look good, or will I seek the true fruitfulness that only comes by a life of abiding in Jesus?

Epilogue

"As a magnifying glass concentrates the rays of the sun into a little burning knot of heat that can set fire to a dry leaf or a piece of paper, so the mystery of Christ in the Gospel concentrates the rays of God's light and fire to a point that sets fire to the spirit of man."[135]

Pursuing the mystery of Christ comes from an insatiable desire to know him more: beyond information to deep experience; beyond expectations built upon my all-too-limited rationality to the growing wonder of this eternal, infinite One. This pursuit leads me back and forth, in and out, between his transcendence—his Otherness beyond all that I will *ever* comprehend—and his immanence: the One who is "closer to me than I am to myself." He is the One who never distances, who only embraces and includes me in himself. He is unconditional and unchanging love, forever and forever. This is at the heart of the mystery and so, as St. Chrysostom wrote,

135 Thomas Merton, *New Seeds of Contemplation,* (New Directions Publishing Co., 2008) p.150

God is love, therefore, love is God. Both surround us, and both are God if we have eyes to see.

Even desiring to know Christ more and to pursue his mysteries is a grace gift from him. It is Christ who puts the spiritual hunger in us; it is him that keeps drawing us further along on this journey. St. Maximus wrote:

> "Questing after this grand mystery was the labor of ancient prophets from Abraham to Zechariah, and now is the vocation of every Christian whose natural intellectual and moral faculties are continually being stretched by the grace of the Holy Spirit."[136]

Notice, Maximus is exhorting those believers who the Holy Spirit has stirred and stretched. In the Scriptures, mystery is a divine secret that is revealed by God in his perfect time for our understanding. Therefore, we trust his timing for placing in us an awareness of mystery and the hunger to pursue it. Pursuing Christ's mysteries is not something that we push ourselves towards; rather, it is a drawing that is initiated by Christ himself.

Earlier, we looked closely at Christ's hypostatic union; at the Incarnation, he became fully God and fully Man, both in One Person. He had two natures, but these were never separated. He was and is always Human and Divine. I stress this because as we consider all that we have examined about the mystery of Christ, it is important that we don't unconsciously slip away from this united understanding. While looking at Christ

---

136 St. Maximus, *On the Cosmic Mystery of Jesus Christ*, (St. Vladimir's Seminary Press, 2003) p.17

beyond time and space, Christ in and before Creation, his presence in and throughout the Old Testament, we are drawn to his Otherness, his Divinity. But in the narrative of the Gospels, when at a literal level we see Christ in his humanity, we must never forget that he is "God from God, light from light, true God from true God."[137] This is why it is so important that we learn to go beyond a literal reading to a deeper, water-to-wine understanding. We see in Jesus' words and actions eternal truths that are revealed, and yet go beyond the Gospels themselves, pointing to the Transcendent and Immanent One. We remember Thomas Merton's words,

> "We read the Gospels not merely to get a picture or
> an idea of Christ but to enter in and pass through
> the words of revelation to establish, by faith, a vital
> contact with the Christ who dwells in our souls as
> God."[138]

* * *

After almost a half century of encountering and walking with Jesus, the past dozen years of truly pursuing the depths of the mystery of Christ have been the greatest adventure of my spiritual life. This pursuit often leads me to exchange my certainties for new questions and wonder. Like St. Maximus, I am "continually being stretched by the grace of the Holy Spirit," as increasingly, Jesus is inviting me in closer, to a greater awareness and experience of my embraced life.

---

137 Nicene Creed
138 Thomas Merton, *Seeds of Contemplation*, p.156

Along the way, I have lost my grip on many of the assumptions I carried for a long time. A Christ who is beyond time and space, for whom the universe he created is merely a reflection of him, is One who cannot be confined by anyone's thoughts and conjectures—no matter how learned or profound they seem.

And so we stop here, for now. When Jesus comes down Mount Olivet, the die is cast. Christ, who lives outside time, space, and matter, has begun to empty himself, choosing a journey that will lead through accusation and death, to the great liberating of captives, and ultimately to the victory of resurrection.

At the Cross we encounter the greatest revelation of the immense love and majesty of Christ. Like the disciples, our pursuit of the Christ mystery must inevitably lead us to the Cross. It is within this mystery where we discover "how wide and long and high and deep is the love of Christ."

Stay tuned for ... *Pursuing the Mystery of the Cross.*

Acknowledgements

Writing this book has been a long and enjoyable journey, beginning a few years before ever I typed the first sentence. Along the way I have received encouragement, insights, adjustments, and for several, the willingness to read multiple edits.

Brad, you are a great friend, mentor, and model. Your influence goes far beyond any book. You have directed me to men and women of the historic faith, opening the way to deep waters with Jesus.

Cherith, thank you for all of the conversations, insights and input. With affection, humor, and always great enthusiasm, you have helped me keep growing in my understanding of what it means to follow the One who is always fully human and fully God.

Brian, thank you for your willingness, in the midst of many demands upon your time, to write the foreword to this book. Through our discussions, your visits to our podcast, and your books, you have steadily expanded my understanding and love for the Gospels.

Christina, thank you for the hours you have given to listening as I read out passages (sometimes entire chapters!), and your willingness to be a sounding board as the ideas behind this book were slowly formed. Your patience is astounding.

Craig, you are the Lord's gift to me. Your encouragement and relentless positivity continue to be a great strength. Thanks for your feedback along the way. I know you are always in my corner, cheering me on.

Tim, your ability to spin so many plates at once is a wonder. Your gifting and passion continue to carry Impact Nations to levels I could have never foreseen. And in the midst of this, you have repeatedly taken time to help me with the complicated process of bringing a book to print.

Susan, thanks for helping and teaching me how to connect a book to the people that I hope will read it.

I am thankful for the Impact Nations staff who, in a variety of ways, have come alongside with practical help throughout the writing process.

Don, once again you agreed to jump into the huge project of line editing another of my books. This one took a lot more time, energy, and focused concentration than any of the others. You have a unique gift for doing this, but I know it comes down to great effort. Thanks for the many hours and days that you put into making this happen.

About Impact Nations

Founded in 2005, Impact Nations partners with leaders in the developing world to rescue lives and transform communities by engaging people in practical and supernatural expressions of the Kingdom of God.

This has led to thousands of children being freed from slavery, hundreds of thousands receiving clean water and food, thousands of single mothers and vulnerable young adults receiving vocational training and employment opportunities, and countless people turning to Christ.

We accomplish our mission primarily through three types of activity:
- Journeys of Compassion
- Relief Efforts
- Skills and Business Training

To learn more about Impact Nations and how you can get involved, contact us:

1-877-736-0803

www.impactnations.com

info@impactnations.com

PO Box 45596
Rio Rancho, NM 87124

More from Steve Stewart

WHEN EVERYTHING CHANGES

The Kingdom of God is bigger, more powerful and more inclusive than we ever imagined. Jesus Christ delcared a gospel that is radical in its scope and implications, and power enough to bring change to everything it touches.

THE JOURNEY

Take a Journey through 35 stories spanninig 25 years and five continents, each one life changing. Steve shares his experiences with a God who is always on the move, rescuing lives and surprising us with His miraculous, extravagant love.

THE FIRST CHURCH RESTORED

Join others who have found the vitality of the Great Commission in their lives and all those they touch. Step into the power, delight and abundance that Jesus promised His church.

To order these titles and more, visit:

www.impactnations.com/shop

impactnations
— rescuing lives
PODCAST

Book an Impact Weekend

Are you looking for a fresh release of Kingdom activity in your community? Host Steve for a life-changing weekend!

Steve teaches scriptural principles, always with an emphasis on practical application. His goal is that people go home not only with more understanding, but more faith and tangible experience than when they arrived. He does this through demonstration and activation/participation. During an *Impact Weekend*, Steve teaches, then provides opportunities for all participants to immediately engage in healing ministry – he takes people out into the community to pray for the sick, share the Gospel and minister to the poor.

Topics include:

- Understanding, Experiencing, and Releasing the Kingdom of God
- The Compassionate Jesus
- Keys to Healing
- Following Jesus
- Justice, the Poor, and the Revolutionary Gospel of Jesus
- The Unsearchable Riches of Christ
- The Power of Inclusion

To to learn more about planning an Impact Weekend in your community, contact us at:

info@impactnations.com

or

1-877-736-0803